60 Quick Knits for Little Kids

PLAYFUL KNITS FOR SIZES 2–6 IN **PACIFIC** AND **PACIFIC** CHUNKY FROM **CASCADE YARNS**

THE EDITORS OF SIXTH&SPRING BOOKS

sixth&springbooks NEW YORK

sixth&springbooks

161 Avenue of the Americas, New York, NY 10013
sixthandspring.com

Editor
PAMELA WYNNE
BUTLER

Vice President/
Editorial Director
TRISHA MALCOLM

Art Director
JOE VIOR

Publisher
CAROLINE KILMER

Yarn Editor
MATTHEW SCHRANK

Production Manager
DAVID JOINNIDES

Editorial Assistant
JACOB SEIFERT

President
ART JOINNIDES

Supervising Patterns
Editor
CARLA SCOTT

Chairman
JAY STEIN

Patterns Editors
PAT HARSTE
RENEE LORION
MARI LYNN PATRICK
SANDI PROSSER

Photography
JACK DEUTSCH

Stylist
JOSEFINA GARCIA

Hair and Makeup
ELENA LYAKIR

CASCADE YARNS
DISTRIBUTOR OF FINE YARN

cascadeyarns.com

Library of Congress Cataloging-in-Publication Data

Names: Sixth & Spring Books, editor. | Cascade Yarns.
Title: 60 quick knits for little kids : playful knits for sizes 2-6 in Pacific and Pacific Chunky from Cascade Yarns / by the editors of Sixth&Spring Books.
Other titles: Sixty quick knits for little kids
Description: First edition. | New York : Sixth&Spring Books, [2016] | Includes index.
Identifiers: LCCN 2016003191 | ISBN 9781942021650 (pbk.)
Subjects: LCSH: Knitting--Patterns. | Children's clothing.
Classification: LCC TT825 .A1255 2016 | DDC 746.43/2--dc23
LC record available at https://lccn.loc.gov/2016003191

Manufactured in China
1 3 5 7 9 10 8 6 4 2
First Edition

contents

From Playground to Preschool

The best-selling *60 Quick Knits* series returns with 60 brand-new patterns created especially for little kids.

In these pages, you'll find dozens of designs for kids ages 2–6 and for every level of knitting experience. From functional to fancy, from the park to classroom, these garments, accessories, and blankets are fun and quick to knit, with bold colors and whimsical motifs sure to be favorites with kids and parents alike.

Each project in this collection was designed using Cascade's *Pacific* and *Pacific Chunky* yarns. Pacific is a soft, strong, easy-care blend of acrylic and superwash merino wool that comes in a brilliant range of colors—perfect for active kids and the adults who care for them.

 To locate retailers that carry Cascade *Pacific*, visit cascadeyarns.com.

Smocked Pinafore

Fastened with ties at the shoulders,
this sweet pinafore looks fancy but is comfy for active tots.

DESIGNED BY CANDACE EISNER STRICK

Sizes
Instructions are written for sizes 2 (4, 6).
Shown in size 4.

Knitted Measurements
Lower edge 40 (42, 44½)"/101.5
(106.5, 113)cm
Chest 20 (22, 24)"/51 (56, 61)cm
Length (excluding ties) 17¾ (19¼,
20¾)"/45 (49, 52.5)cm

Materials
■ 3 (3, 4) 3½oz/100g skeins (each
approx 213yd/195m) of Cascade Yarns
Pacific (acrylic/superwash merino wool) in
#51 Honeysuckle Pink (4)
■ Size 6 (4mm) circular needle, 24"/60cm
long, *or size to obtain gauge*
■ One pair size 6 (4mm) needles
■ Spare size 6 (4mm) needle
■ Stitch holders
■ Stitch markers

Notes
1) Bottom borders are worked back and
forth in rows.
2) Skirt is worked in the round.
3) Front and back bodices are worked
back and forth in rows.

Stitch Glossary
Selvage st Slip first st purlwise with yarn
in front, move yarn to back between
needles before working next st.

Smocking Pattern
(over a multiple of 6 sts plus 3)
Row 1 and all WS rows Purl.
Row 2 (RS) K2, *wyif slip 5 sts purlwise,

k1; rep from *, end k1.
Row 4 K4, *insert RH needle under
strand and k next st, bringing the new
stitch under the strand, k5; rep from *,
end last rep k4.
Row 6 K1, wyif slip 3 sts purlwise, *k1,
wyif slip 5 sts purlwise; rep from *, end
last rep, k1, wyif slip 3 sts purlwise, k1.
Row 8 K1, *k next st with strand as in
row 4, k5; rep from *, end last rep k1.
Rep rows 1–8 for smocking pat.

Front Hem
With straight needles, cast on 105 (111,
117) sts.
Next row Selvage st, k to end.
Rep this row 4 times more.

BEGIN SMOCKING PATTERN
Row 1 (WS) Selvage st, k2, pm, work
row 1 of smocking pat over next 99 (105,
111) sts, pm, k3.
Row 2 (RS) Selvage st, k2, sm, work row
2 of smocking pat to next marker, sm, k3.
Keeping 3 sts each side in garter st (k
every row as established, cont to work
rows 3–8 of smocking pat, then rep 1–8
once more, then rows 1–5, end with a
WS row.
Do *not* bind off. Leave sts on spare needle.

Gauge
21 sts and 28 rnds to 4"/10cm over St st using size 6 (4mm) circular needle.
Take time to check gauge.

Smocked **1** Pinafore

Back Hem
Repeat as for front hem.

Skirt
With circular needle, join front and back hems as foll:
Next rnd K105 (111, 117) sts of front hem, pm, k105 (111, 117) sts of back hem—210 (222, 234) sts.
Join and pm for beg of rnd.

Next 5 rnds [Purl 1 rnd, knit 1 rnd] twice, purl 1 rnd.
Work in St st (knit every rnd) as foll:
Dec rnd K2tog, k to 2 sts before next marker, ssk, sm, k2tog, k to 2 sts before beg rnd marker, ssk, sm.
Rep dec rnd every 5th (6th, 6th) rnd 11 times more—162 (174, 186) sts.
Work even until piece measures 13 (14, 15)"/33 (35.5, 38)cm from beg.
Dec rnd *K10 (11, 12), [k2tog] 30 (32, 34) times, k11 (12, 13); rep from * once more—102 (110, 118) sts.
Next 5 rnds [Purl 1 rnd, knit 1 rnd] twice, purl 1 rnd.

Divide for front and back bodices as foll:
Next rnd K to last 5 (5, 6) sts of rnd, bind off next 10 (10, 12) sts, dropping marker, k until there are 41 (45, 47) sts on RH needle (front bodice), bind off next 10 (10, 12) sts, dropping marker, k until there are another 41 (45, 47) sts on RH needle (back bodice). Cut yarn.

Front Bodice
With straight needles, work back and forth in rows as foll:
Next row (RS) Selvage st, k3 (2, 3), pm, work row 2 of smocking pat over next 33 (39, 39) sts, pm, k4 (3, 4).

Leave rem 41 (45, 47) sts on circular needle for back bodice.
Next row (WS) Selvage st, k2, p1 (0, 1), sm, work row 3 of smocking pat to next marker, sm, p1 (0, 1), k3.
Keeping 4 (3, 4) sts each side in pat sts as established, cont to work rows 4–8 of smocking pat, then rep rows 1–8 for 2 (2, 3) times more, then rows 1–4 for 0 (1, 0) times, end with a RS row.
Next row (WS) Selvage st, k to end. Rep this row 6 times more, end with a WS row.
Next row (RS) Selvage st, k2, place these 3 sts on st holder for tie, bind off next 35 (39, 41) sts, k to end—3 sts (first tie).

TIES
Next row Selvage st, k2 to end.
Rep this row until tie measures 4 (4½, 5)"/10 (11.5, 12.5)cm.
Next row K3tog. Fasten off last st.
Transfer 3 sts on holder to straight needle ready for a WS row. Work as for first tie.

Back Bodice
With RS facing, work as for front bodice.

Finishing
Block piece to measurements.
To wear, tie at shoulders. ■

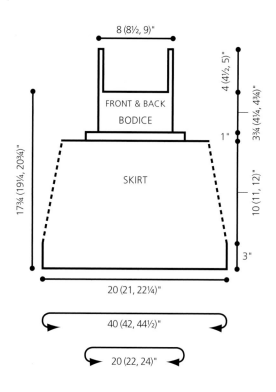

8 (8½, 9)"

4 (4½, 5)"

3¾ (4¼, 4¾)"

FRONT & BACK BODICE

1"

17¾ (19¼, 20¾)"

SKIRT

10 (11, 12)"

3"

20 (21, 22¼)"

40 (42, 44½)"

20 (22, 24)"

Chunky Turtleneck

Fast and fun in neon orange, this easy-knit pullover sports a close-fit turtleneck and patterned yoke.

DESIGNED BY AUDREY DRYSDALE

Sizes
Instructions are written for sizes 2 (4, 6). Shown in size 4.

Knitted Measurements
Chest 26 (28, 30)"/66 (71, 76)cm
Length 13½ (14½, 15¾)"/34.5 (37, 40)cm
Upper arm 10 (10½, 11)"/25.5 (26.5, 28)cm

Materials
■ 3 (4, 5) 3½oz/100 g skeins (each approx 120yd/110m) of Cascade Yarns *Pacific Chunky* (acrylic/superwash merino wool) in #84 Neon Orange ⑤
■ One pair each sizes 10 and 10½ (6 and 6.5mm) needles, *or size to obtain gauge*
■ Stitch markers
■ Stitch holders

K1, P1 Rib
(over an odd number of sts)
Row 1 (RS) *K1, p1; rep from *, end k1.
Row 2 *P1, k1; rep from *, end p1.
Rep rows 1 and 2 for k1, p1 rib.

Seed Stitch
(over an odd number of sts)
Row 1 (RS) P1, *k1, p1; rep from * to end.
Row 2 K the purl sts and p the knit sts.
Rep row 2 for seed st.

Back
With smaller needles, cast on 45 (49, 53) sts. Work in k1, p1 rib for 2"/5cm. Change to larger needles.
Cont in St st (k on RS, p on WS) until piece measures 8¼ (9, 10)"/21 (23, 25.5)cm from beg.

ARMHOLE SHAPING
Bind off 3 sts at beg of next 2 rows.
Dec 1 st each side of next RS row then every other row 0 (1, 2) times more —37 (39, 41) sts.
Work 1 row even.

BEGIN SEED STITCH YOKE
Next row (RS) K15 (16, 17), pm, p1, [k1, p1] 3 times, pm, k to end.
Next row P to 1 st before the marker, place new marker. Removing previous markers, k1, [p1, k1] 4 times, place new marker, p to end.
Next row K to 1 st before the marker, place new marker. Removing previous markers, work seed st over 11 sts, place new marker, k to end.
Next row P to 1 st before the marker, place new marker. Removing previous markers, work seed st over 13 sts, place new marker, p to end.
Rep the last 2 rows, adding 1 new st in seed st each side of the previously worked seed sts, until all sts are worked in seed st. Cont in seed st until armhole measures 5¼ (5½, 5¾)"/13.5 (14, 14.5)cm.

NECK AND SHOULDERS
Bind off 9 (10, 10) sts, work 19 (19, 21)

Gauge
14 sts and 18 rows to 4"/10cm over St st using larger needles.
Take time to check gauge

Chunky Turtleneck

sts in pat and place these sts on holder, bind off rem 9 (10, 10) sts.

Front
Work same as back until armhole measures 3½ (3¾, 4)"/9 (9.5, 10)cm.

NECK SHAPING
Next row (RS) Work 14 (15, 15) sts in pat, sl the center 9 (9, 11) sts to holder, join a 2nd ball of yarn and work to end. Working both sides at once, dec 1 st at each neck edge every row 4 times, then every 2nd row once more—9 (10, 10) sts rem each side. Work each side even until armhole measures same as back. Bind off rem sts each side.

Sleeves
With smaller needles, cast on 27 (29, 31) sts. Work in k1, p1 rib for 3"/7.5cm. Change to larger needles and, beg with a RS row, work 4 rows in St st.
Inc row (RS) K1, kfb, k to last 2 sts, kfb, k1. Rep inc row every 8th row 3 times more—35 (37, 39) sts.
Work even until piece measures 10½ (12, 13¼)"/26.5 (30.5, 34)cm from beg.

CAP SHAPING
Bind off 3 sts at beg of next 10 rows. Bind off rem 5 (7, 9) sts.

Finishing
Block pieces to measurements. Sew right shoulder seam.

TURTLENECK
With RS facing and smaller needles, pick up and k 12 sts from shaped front neck edge, k9 (9, 11) sts from front holder, pick up and k 12 sts from other shaped front neck edge, k19 (19, 21) sts from back neck holder while inc 1 st at center of these back neck sts—53 (53, 57) sts. Beg with row 2 of rib, work in k1, p1 rib for 5"/12.5cm. Bind off in rib using larger needle.
Sew left shoulder seam, then the turtleneck seam with the top half sewn so the seam is hidden when the collar is folded down.
Sew sleeves into armholes.
Sew side and sleeve seams.
Fold back cuffs as shown in photo. ∎

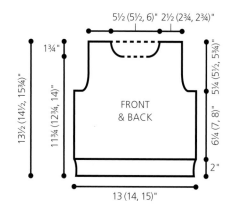

5½ (5½, 6)" 2½ (2¾, 2¾)"

1¾"

13½ (14½, 15¾)"

11¾ (12¾, 14)"

5¼ (5½, 5¾)"

6¼ (7, 8)"

FRONT & BACK

2"

13 (14, 15)"

10 (10½, 11)"

2¼"

7½ (9, 10½)"

SLEEVE

3"

7¾ (8¼, 9)"

Square Cap

Jaunty tassels top this tweed cap, knit in a slip-stitch pattern that looks complex but is simple to work.

DESIGNED BY ELLEN LIGUORI

Sizes
Instructions are written for sizes Baby (Toddler, Child). Shown in size Baby.

Knitted Measurements
Brim circumference 14½ (16, 18)"/37 (40.5, 45.5)cm
Length 6½ (7½, 8½)"/16.5 (19, 21.5)cm

Materials
■ 1 3½oz/100g skein (each approx 213yd/195m) of Cascade Yarns *Pacific* (acrylic/superwash merino wool) each in #20 Baby Blue (A) and #46 Lapis (B) (🧶4🧶)
■ One pair each sizes 6 and 7 (4 and 4.5mm) needles, *or size to obtain gauge*
■ Stitch marker

Flecked Tweed Pattern
(over a multiple of 4 sts plus 3)
Row 1 (WS) With B, p1, bring yarn to back and sl 1, bring yarn to front, *p3, bring yarn to back and sl 1, bring yarn to front; rep from * to last st, p1.
Row 2 With B, k1, sl 1 wyib, *k3, sl 1 wyib; rep from * to last st, k1.
Row 3 With A, p3, *bring yarn to back and sl 1, bring yarn to front, p3; rep from * to end.
Row 4 With A, k3, *sl 1 wyib, k3; rep from * to end.
Rep rows 1–4 for flecked tweed pat.

Cap
With smaller needles and A, cast on 79 (87, 99) sts.
Row 1 (RS) K1, *p1, k1; rep from * to end.
Row 2 P1, *k1, p1; rep from * to end.
Rep rows 1 and 2 for k1, p1 rib twice more, then rep row 1 once more.
Change to larger needles.
Work in flecked tweed pattern until piece measures 6½ (7½, 8½)"/16.5 (19, 21.5)cm from beg, end with a RS row. Bind off.

Finishing
Place marker at center of bound-off edge. Fold hat in half widthwise, with RS facing, and sew center back seam with A. Turn hat inside out and align center back seam with marker. With A, sew top seam, working through inside loops of each stitch along bound-off edge. Holding A and B together, make 2 tassels approx 3½"/9cm long. Secure one tassel to each corner of hat. Weave in ends. ■

Gauge
22 sts and 26 rows to 4"/10cm over flecked tweed pat using larger needles. *Take time to check gauge.*

Silver and Gold Blanket

Bold blocks of color march across this garter-stitch blanket, worked either in two panels or in one seamless piece.

DESIGNED BY AUDREY DRYSDALE

Knitted Measurements
35 x 35"/89 x 89cm

Materials
- 4 3½oz/100g skeins (each approx 120yd/110m) of Cascade Yarns *Pacific Chunky* (acrylic/superwash merino wool) in #02 White (A) **⑤**
- 2 skeins each in #13 Gold (B) and #61 Silver (C)
- One pair size 10 (6mm) needles, or one circular needle, 32"/80cm long (if making in one piece), *or size to obtain gauge*
- Stitch markers
- Tapestry needle

Notes
1) Blanket is written in 2 versions. Version 1 works the blanket in two separate panels that are sewn tog. Version 2 works the blanket in one piece, changing colors at the center for the B and C stripes.
2) If working the blanket in one piece, use a circular needle to accommodate the large number of sts. Do *not* join.
3) If working the blanket in one piece, when changing colors, twist yarns on WS to prevent holes in work.

Blanket—Version 1 (two separate panels)
Panel 1
With B, cast on 55 sts.
Beg with a WS row, knit 15 rows in garter st (k every row), end with a WS row.
[With A, knit 16 rows; with B, knit 16 rows] 6 times. With B, bind off.

Panel 2
With C, cast on 55 sts.
Beg with a WS row, knit 15 rows in garter st, end with a WS row.
[With A, knit 16 rows; with C, knit 16 rows] 6 times. With C, bind off.

Finishing
Sew panels together at center seam, matching stripes. Weave in ends.

Blanket—Version 2 (made in one piece)
With B, cast on 55 sts; with C, cast on 55 sts—110 sts.
Next row (WS) K55 C, k55 B.
Next 14 rows Cont in garter st, matching colors, end with a WS row.
*****Next 16 rows** With A, k all sts.
Next row (RS) K55 B, k55 C.
Next 15 rows Cont in garter st, matching colors, end with a WS row.
Rep from * 5 times more.
Bind off, matching colors.

Finishing
Weave in ends. ∎

Gauge
12 sts and 24 rows to 4"/10cm over garter st using size 10 (6mm) needles.
Take time to check gauge.

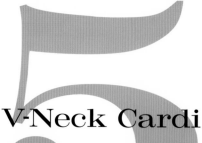

V-Neck Cardi

Liven up a classic cardigan with chunky details
and an unexpected stripe pattern.

DESIGNED BY KIRI FITZGERALD-HILLIER

Sizes
Instructions are written for sizes 2 (4, 6).
Shown in size 4.

Knitted Measurements
Chest (closed) 25½ (27½, 29½)"/64.5
(69.6, 75)cm
Length 13½ (14½, 15¾)"/34 (37, 40)cm
Upper arm 9¼ (10, 10¾)"/23.5 (25.5, 27)cm

Materials
■ 2 3½oz/100g skeins (each approx
213yd/195m) of Cascade Yarns *Pacific*
(acrylic/superwash merino wool) in
#9 Sand (MC) (4)
■ 1 skein each #65 Denim Heather (A)
and #101 Red Orange (B)
■ One each sizes 6 and 7 (4 and 4.5mm)
circular needle, 24"/60cm long,
or size to obtain gauge
■ One set (5) each sizes 6 and 7 (4 and
4.5mm) double-pointed needles (dpn)
■ Four 1"/25mm buttons
■ Stitch markers
■ Stitch holders

Notes
1) Cardi is knit from the top down.
2) Circular needles are used on the body
to accommodate the large number of sts.
Do *not* join. Work back and forth in rows.
3) Sleeves are worked in the round using dpn.

Stripe Pattern
Worked in St st (k on RS, p on WS) as foll:
12 rows MC, 2 rows A, 1 row MC, 1 row B,
1 row MC, 2 rows A, 8 rows MC, 2 rows B,
1 row MC, 1 row A, 1 row MC, 2 rows B,
18 rows MC, 2 rows A, 1 row MC, 1 row B,
1 row MC, 2 rows A.
Rep these 59 rows for stripe pat.

Stitch Glossary
M1R (make 1 right) Insert LH needle from
back to front under the strand between
last st worked and next st on LH needle.
K into the front loop to twist the st.
M1L (make 1 left) Insert LH needle from
front to back under the strand between
last st worked and next st on LH needle.
K into the back loop to twist the st.

One-Row Buttonhole
With yarn in front, sl next st purlwise,
bring yarn to back, [sl next st purlwise,
pass 2nd st on RH needle over first st] 2
times, slip last st from RH needle back to
LH needle, turn work, cast on 3 sts using
cable cast-on, turn work back and slip
first st from LH needle to RH needle, pass
2nd st on RH needle over first st.

Gauge
20 sts and 28 rows at 4"/10cm over St st using larger needles.
Take time to check gauge.

V-Neck Cardi

Cardi
Beg at the neck edge, with larger circular needle and MC, cast on 56 sts.

Set-up row (WS) P1 (left front), pm, p4 (armhole sts), pm, p6 (left sleeve), pm, p4 (armhole sts), pm, p26 (back), pm, p4 (armhole sts), pm, p6 (right sleeve), pm, p4 (armhole sts), pm, p1 (right front). Work in St st and stripe pat as foll:

Inc row 1 (RS) [K to marker, M1L, sm, k4, sm, M1R] 4 times, k to end—8 sts inc'd for armholes.

Row 2 Purl.
Rep last 2 rows twice more—80 sts.

Inc row 7 (RS) K1, M1R (neck inc), [k to marker, M1L, sm, k4, sm, M1R] 4 times, k to last st, M1L (neck inc), k1—8 sts inc'd for armholes, 2 sts inc'd for neck, for a total of 10 sts inc'd.

Row 8 Purl.
Row 9 Rep inc row 1.
Row 10 Purl.
Rep last 4 rows (rows 7–10) for 5 (6, 7) times more then rep rows 7 and 8 once more—198 (216, 234) sts.

DIVIDE FOR BODY AND SLEEVES
Note Make note of where you are in the stripe pattern for the sleeves. Remove markers as you come to them on first row.

Row 1 (RS) K26 (29, 32) for right front, place next 42 (46, 50) sts on holder for right sleeve, cast on 2 sts, k62 (66, 70) for back, place next 42 (46, 50) sts on holder for left sleeve, cast on 2 sts, k26 (29, 32) for left front—118 (128, 138) sts for body.

Row 2 Purl.
Row 3 K1, M1R, k to 1 st before end, M1L, k1—120 (130, 140) sts.
Cont in St st and stripe pat until piece measures 6½ (7, 7½)"/16.5 (18, 19)cm from dividing row, end with a WS row.

Change to A and knit next row on RS, dec 1 (5, 3) sts evenly across row—119 (125, 137) sts.
Change to smaller needles.

Next row (WS) P4, *k3, p3; rep from * to last 7 sts, k3, p4.

Next row K the knit sts and p the purl sts.
Rep last row for k3, p3 rib for 1¾"/4.5cm, end with a WS row.
Bind off in rib, leaving last st on needle for first st of front band.

FRONTS AND NECK BAND
With RS facing, smaller needle and A, pick up and k 201 (213, 231) sts evenly along right front, back neck and left front edge.

Row 1 (WS) *P3, k3; rep from * to last 3 sts, p3.

Row 2 K the knit sts and p the purl sts.
Rep last row for k3, p3 rib for 5 rows more.
For boys only

Row 8 (RS) Cont in rib to last 45 sts, [work one-row buttonhole, p3, k3, p3] 3 times, work one-row buttonhole, p3, k3.
For girls only

Row 8 (RS) K3, p3, [work one-row buttonhole, p3, k3, p3] 3 times, work one-row buttonhole, cont in rib to end.
For boys and girls
Work even in rib for 5 rows more.
Bind off in rib.

Sleeves
Cont stripe pat to match body, use larger dpn to pick up and k 2 sts from underarm, k42 (46, 50) sts from holder, pick up and k 2 sts, pm, join to work in rnds—46 (50, 54) sts.

Dec rnd K1, k2tog, k to last 3 sts, ssk, k1—2 sts dec'd.
Knit 5 (7, 5) rnds.
Rep last 6 (8, 6) rnds 6 (5, 7) times more, then rep dec rnd once more—30 (36, 36) sts. Work even until sleeve measures 6½ (7½, 8½)"/16.5 (19, 21.5)cm from dividing row.
Change to smaller needles and MC, knit 1 rnd.

Next rnd *K3, p3; rep from * around.
Rep last rnd until rib measures 2½ (3½, 3½)"/6.5 (9, 9)cm. Bind off in rib.

Finishing
Block to measurements. Sew on buttons opposite buttonholes. ■

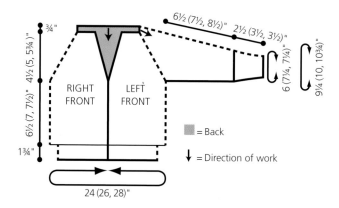

Textured Tunic

Daisy stitch forms bouquets at the hem of this A-line tunic,
then scatters like seeds over the body and three-quarter-length sleeves.

DESIGNED BY CAARIN FLEISCHMANN

Sizes
Instructions are written for sizes 2 (4, 6).
Shown in size 4.

Knitted Measurements
Chest 26 (28, 30)"/66 (71, 76)cm
Length 14½ (15, 16)"/37 (38, 40.5)cm
Upper arm 8 (9, 10)"/20.5 (23, 25.5)cm

Materials
■ 2 (2, 3) 3½oz/100g skeins (each
approx 213yd/195m) of Cascade Yarns
Pacific (acrylic/superwash merino wool)
in #16 Spring Green (4)
■ One pair each sizes 5 and 6 (3.75 and
4mm) needles, *or size to obtain gauge*

Stitch Glossary
MD (make daisy) P3tog but do *not*
drop sts off LH needle, yo (wrapping yarn
completely around needle), p same 3 sts
tog again, dropping sts from the needle.

Daisy Pattern Stitch
(over a multiple of 4 sts plus 3)
Rows 1 and 3 (RS) Knit.
Row 2 (WS) P1, k1, *MD, k1; rep from
* to last st, p1.
Row 4 P1, k1, p1, k1, *MD, k1; rep from
* to last 3 sts, p1, k1, p1.
Rep rows 1–4 for daisy pat st.

Back
With smaller needles, cast on 75 (79,
83) sts. Knit 2 rows. Change to larger
needles and work in daisy pat st for
24 rows, dec 1 st at end of the last WS
row—74 (78, 82) sts.

BEGIN CHART PATTERN
Row 1 (RS) Knit.

Row 2 (WS) P5 (2, 2), work the 16-st
rep 4 times, then work sts 16–12 (16–5,
16–1) once more. Cont to foll chart in
this way through row 4.
Note When working decs into pat, if
there are not enough sts to work MD,
then work sts in St st (k on RS, p on WS).
Dec row 3 (RS) K1, k2tog, k to last 3 sts,
ssk, k1—2 sts dec'd.
Row 4 Work even in pat.
Dec row 5 Rep dec row 3.
Rows 6–12 Work even in pat.
Dec row 13 Rep dec row 3.
Rows 14–20 Work even in pat.
Dec row 21 Rep dec row 3.
Rows 22–28 Work even in pat.
Dec row 29 Rep dec row 3—64 (68, 72) sts.
Row 30 Purl.
Row 31 Knit.
Cont to rep chart rows 20–31 in pat as
established for 5 rows more.
Next row (RS) Rep dec row 3—62 (66,
70) sts.
Work even, foll the 12-row rep until piece
measures 10 (10, 10½)"/25.5 (25.5, 26.5)
cm from beg.

ARMHOLE SHAPING
Bind off 5 sts at beg of next 2 rows—52
(56, 60) sts. Cont in 12-row rep chart pat

Gauge
19 sts and 27 rows to 4"/10 cm over St st, after blocking, using larger needles.
Take time to check gauge.

Textured Tunic

as established until armhole measures 4 (4½, 5)"/10 (11.5, 12.5)cm.

SHOULDER SHAPING
Bind off 5 (7, 7) sts at beg of next 2 rows, then 5 (5, 7) sts at beg of next 2 rows.
Next row (RS) K1, k2tog, k to the last 3 sts, ssk, k1—30 sts.
Work 4 rows even.
Change to smaller needles. Knit 2 rows.
Bind off.

Front
Work same as back.

Sleeves
With smaller needles, cast on 39 sts.
Knit 2 rows. Change to larger needles and work in daisy pat st for 20 rows, dec 1 st at end of the last WS row—38 sts.

BEGIN CHART PATTERN
Row 1 (RS) Knit.

Row 2 (WS) P6, work the 16-st rep twice. Cont to foll chart in this way through row 10.
Inc row (RS) K1, kfb, k to last 2 sts, kfb, k1.
Note After working through chart row 31, cont to rep rows 20–31 to end of sleeve. Rep inc row every 10th row 0 (2, 4) times more—40 (44, 48) sts.
Work even until piece measures 8½ (10½, 11½)"/21.5 (26.5, 29)cm from beg. Bind off.

Finishing
Block pieces to measurements.
Sew shoulder and neckband seams.
Placing top of sleeve seam at the shoulder seam and with top 1"/2.5 cm of the sleeve fitting into the armhole bind-offs, sew sleeve into armholes.
Sew side and sleeve seams. ■

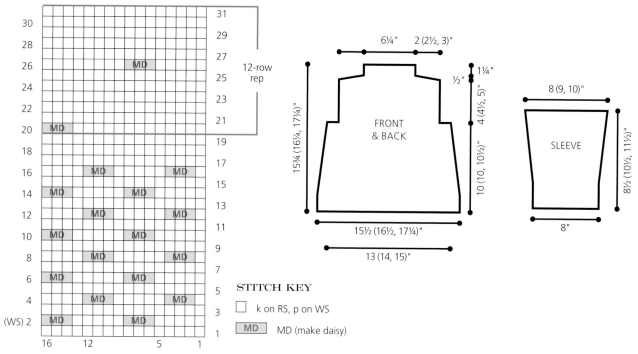

STITCH KEY

☐ k on RS, p on WS

MD MD (make daisy)

Sailor-Stripe Pullover

Stripes ahoy! Set sail in this Breton-inspired raglan,
jazzed up with contrasting trim and an asymmetrical buttonband.

DESIGNED BY YOKO HATTA

Sizes
Instructions are written for sizes 2 (4, 6).
Shown in size 4.

Knitted Measurements
Chest 26 (27, 29)"/66 (68.5, 73.5)cm
Length 14¼ (15½, 16½)"/36 (39.5, 42)cm
Upper arm 10½ (11¼, 12)"/26.5 (28.5, 30.5)cm

Materials
- 2 3½ oz/100 g skeins (each approx 213yd/195m) of Cascade Yarns *Pacific* (acrylic/superwash merino wool) in #02 White (A) ▨
- 1 skein each in #46 Navy (B) and #43 Red (C)
- One pair each sizes 5 and 7 (3.75 and 4.5mm) needles, *or size to obtain gauge*
- Three ⅝"/15mm buttons

Stripe Pattern
Working in St st (k on RS, p on WS), work *2 rows B, 4 rows A; rep from * for the 6-row stripe pat.

Note
One k1 selvage st is worked at all seam edges and is not figured into the finished measurements.

Back
With larger needles and A, cast on 66 (70, 75) sts. Knit 1 row on the WS, purl 1 row on the RS.

Beg with a WS purl row, work in St st for 11 rows more.

BEGIN STRIPE PATTERN
Work the 6-row stripe pattern until piece measures 8¼ (8¾, 9¼)"/21 (22, 23.5)cm from beg.

RAGLAN ARMHOLE SHAPING
Bind off 4 sts at beg of next 2 rows.
Work 2 rows even.
Dec row (RS) K1, ssk, k to last 3 sts, k2tog, k1—2 sts dec'd.
Rep dec row every other row 16 (18, 20) times more—24 (24, 25) sts.
Purl 1 row. Bind off.

Front
Work same as back, including the armhole shaping, until there are 40 (40, 41) sts, pm to mark center 12 (12, 13) sts on last WS row.

NECK SHAPING
Next row (RS) K1, ssk, k to center marked sts, join a 2nd ball of yarn and

Gauge
20 sts and 27 rows to 4"/10cm over St st using larger needles. *Take time to check gauge.*

7
Sailor-Stripe Pullover

bind off center 12 (12, 13) sts, k to last 3 sts, k2tog, k1.

Working both sides at once, cont to work raglan shaping every RS row 4 times more and, AT THE SAME TIME, bind off 4 sts from each neck edge once, 2 sts once, then 1 st once. Fasten off rem 2 sts each side.

Right Sleeve

With larger needles and A, cast on 32 (34, 38) sts. Knit 1 row on the WS, purl 1 row on the RS.

Beg with a WS purl row, work in St st for 11 rows more.

BEGIN STRIPE PATTERN

Work the 6-row stripe pattern, inc 1 st each side of first row then every 6th row 0 (4, 7) times more, then every 4th row 10 (7, 4) times more—54 (58, 62) sts. Work even until piece measures 8¼ (10¼, 11¼)"/21 (26, 28.5) cm from beg.

RAGLAN CAP SHAPING

Bind off 4 sts at beg of next 2 rows. Work 2 rows even.

Dec row (RS) K1, ssk, k to last 3 sts, k2tog, k1—2 sts dec'd.

Rep dec row every other row 13 (15, 17) times more—18 sts. Purl 1 row.

TOP OF CAP SHAPING

Next row (RS) Bind off 9 sts, k to last 3 sts, k2tog, k1—8 sts.

Purl 1 row.

Next row Bind off 2 sts, k to last 3 sts, k2tog, k1—5 sts.

Purl 1 row.

Next row K3tog, k2tog.

Purl 1 row. Bind off rem 2 sts.

Left Sleeve

Work as for right sleeve to top of cap shaping, ending with a RS row—18 sts.

TOP OF CAP SHAPING

Next row (WS) Bind off 9 sts, purl to end—9 sts.

Next row K1, ssk, k to end—8 sts.

Next row Bind off 2 sts, purl to end—6 sts.

Next row K1, ssk, k to end—5 sts.

Next row (WS) Bind off 2 sts, purl to end—3 sts.

Next row K1, ssk.

Bind off rem 2 sts.

Finishing

Block pieces to measurements on the WS. Sew raglan seams into armholes, leaving the left front seam open.

NECKBAND

With smaller needles and C, pick up and k 84 (84, 86) sts around neck opening. Knit 5 rows. Bind off.

LEFT FRONT SLEEVE TRIM

With smaller needles and A, pick up and k 28 (31, 34) sts from the left front sleeve opening. Knit 3 rows. Bind off.

LEFT FRONT TRIM

With smaller needles and C, pick up and k 28 (31, 34) sts from the left front raglan edge opening. Knit 1 row.

Buttonhole row (RS) K5 (6, 6), [k2tog, yo, k8 (9, 10)] twice, k2tog, yo, k1 (1, 2). Knit 3 rows. Bind off. Sew side and sleeve seams. Sew buttons opposite buttonholes. ∎

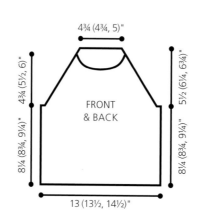

FRONT & BACK

4¾ (4¾, 5)"

4¾ (5½, 6)"

5½ (6¼, 6¾)"

8¼ (8¾, 9¼)"

8¼ (8¾, 9¼)"

13 (13½, 14½)"

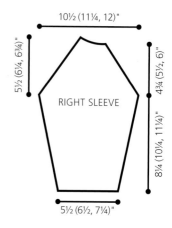

RIGHT SLEEVE

10½ (11¼, 12)"

5½ (6¼, 6¾)"

4¾ (5½, 6)"

8¼ (10¼, 11¼)"

5½ (6½, 7¼)"

Zigzag Dress

Inspired by Guernsey sweaters, this neutral dress is perfect
for layering over long sleeves and leggings.

DESIGNED BY LISA CRAIG

Sizes
Instructions are written for sizes 2 (4, 6).
Shown in size 6.

Knitted Measurements
Chest 22 (24, 26)"/56 (61, 66)cm
Length 16½ (18½, 21)"/42 (47, 53)cm

Materials
▪ 2 (3, 3) 3½oz/100g skeins (each
approx 213yd/195m) of Cascade Yarns
Pacific (acrylic/superwash merino wool)
in #61 Silver
▪ One pair each sizes 7 and 8 (4.5 and
5mm) needles, *or size to obtain gauge*
▪ Size 7 (4.5mm) circular needle,
16"/40cm long
▪ Stitch holders
▪ Stitch marker

Back
With smaller needle, cast on 65 (73, 81) sts.
Work 6 rows in garter stitch (k every row).
Change to larger needles and work 4
rows in St st (k on RS, p on WS).

BEGIN ZIGZAG CHART
Row 1 (RS) Work the 8-st rep 8 (9, 10)
times, work the last st of chart. Cont to

foll chart in this way through row 36.
Cont in St st until piece measures 10½
(12, 14)"/26.5 (30.5, 35.5)cm from beg,
end with a WS row.
Dec row (RS) K14 (10, 10), k2tog, [k2,
k2tog] 4 (6, 7) times, k1, [SKP, k2] 4 (6,
7) times, [SKP] 1 (0, 1) times, k12 (12,
10)—55 (60, 65) sts.
Work 7 rows even in St st.

ARMHOLE SHAPING
Bind off 3 sts at beg of next 2 rows.
Dec 1 st each side of next row then *every*
row 4 (6, 6) times more—39 (40, 45) sts.
Work even until armhole measures 4¾
(5¼, 5¾)"/12 (13.5, 14.5)cm.

NECK SHAPING
Next row (RS) K8 (8, 9), turn, leaving
rem sts on needle.
Next row (WS) Bind off 2 sts, purl to end.
Bind off 6 (6, 7) sts for right shoulder.
Next row (RS) Sl center 23 (24, 27) sts
to holder, rejoin yarn to last 8 (8, 9) sts,
bind off 2 sts, k to end.
Next row P6 (6, 7).
Bind off 6 (6, 7) sts for left shoulder.

Front
Work same as back until armhole measures
1 (1½, 2)"/2.5 (4, 5) cm—39 (40, 45) sts.

NECK SHAPING
Next row (RS) K14 (14, 15), turn, leaving
rem sts on needle.
Next row Purl.
Dec row K to last 2 sts, k2tog.
Rep dec row every other row 7 times
more—6 (6, 7) sts rem.

Gauge
20 sts and 27 rows to 4"/10cm over St st using larger needles.
Take time to check gauge.

Zigzag Dress

Work even until armhole measures same as back. Bind off rem sts for left shoulder.
Next row (RS) Sl center 11 (12, 15) sts to holder, rejoin yarn to last 14 (14, 15) sts, k to end.
Next row (WS) Purl.
Dec row SKP, k to end.
Rep dec row every other row 7 times more—6 (6, 7) sts rem.
Complete as for left shoulder.

Finishing
Weave in ends and block pieces.
Sew shoulder seams.

ARMHOLE TRIM
With RS facing and smaller needles, pick up and k 64 (70, 76) sts evenly around armhole.
Work 6 rows garter st. Bind off. Rep for other armhole.
Sew side seams.

NECKBAND
With RS facing and circular needle, pick up and k 2 sts from shaped back neck edge, k23 (24, 27) sts from holder, pick up and k 2 sts from shaped back neck and 23 sts from shaped front neck edge, k11 (12, 15) sts from front holder, pick up and k 23 sts from shaped front neck edge—84 (86, 92) sts.
Join to work in rnds and pm to mark beg of rnd.
[Knit 1 rnd, purl 1 rnd] 3 times. Bind off. ■

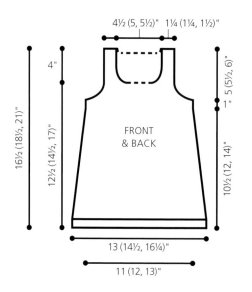

4½ (5, 5½)" 1¼ (1¼, 1½)"

4"

5 (5½, 6)"

1"

16½ (18½, 21)"

12½ (14½, 17)"

10½ (12, 14)"

FRONT & BACK

13 (14½, 16¼)"

11 (12, 13)"

ZIGZAG CHART

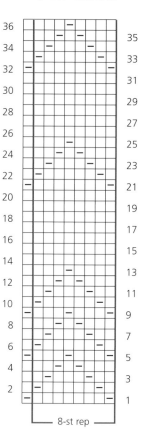

8-st rep

STITCH KEY

☐ k on RS, p on WS

⊟ p on RS, k on WS

Pencil Scarf

Send them off to preschool looking sharp!
This reversible graphic scarf suits kids of all ages.

DESIGNED BY STACEY GERBMAN

Knitted Measurements
Width 5"/12.5cm
Length 36"/91.5cm

Materials
- 1 3½oz/100g skein (each approx 213yd/195m) of Cascade Yarns *Pacific* (acrylic/superwash merino wool) each in #02 White (A), #96 Treetop (B), #13 Gold (C), and #94 Jet Heather (D)
- One set (5) size 7 (4.5mm) double pointed needles (dpn), *or size to obtain gauge*
- Stitch markers

Scarf
ERASER
With A, cast on 52 sts. Divide sts evenly over 4 dpn (13 sts per needle) and join, taking care not to twist sts. Pm for beg of rnd.
Rnd 1 *K1, p1; rep from * around.
Rep rnd 1 for k1, p1 rib for 2½"/6.5cm. Change to B.

FERRULE
With B, [knit 1 rnd, purl 1 rnd] twice. Knit 2 rnds.

Next rnd *K2, p2; rep from * around.
Next rnd Knit.
Rep last 2 rnds three times more.
Knit 2 rnds.
[Purl 1 rnd, knit 1 rnd] twice, knit 1 rnd. Change to C.

PENCIL
With C, work even in St st (k every rnd) until piece measures approx 30"/76cm from beg. Change to A.

TIP
With A, knit 2 rnds.
Next rnd K26, pm, k26.
Dec rnd [K1, ssk, k to 3 sts before marker, k2tog, k1] twice—4 sts dec'd.
Rep dec rnd every 4th rnd six times more—24 sts rem.
Change to D and cont to work dec rnd every 4th rnd four times more—8 sts.

Finishing
Graft tip together. Weave in ends.
Lightly block scarf to measurements. ■

Gauge
20 sts and 26 rnds to 4"/10cm over St st using size 7 (4.5mm) needles.
Take time to check gauge.

Bear Hat

With a soft strap to keep it snugly in place,
this cleverly constructed hat is unbearably cute!

DESIGNED BY BEA NARETTO

Knitted Measurements
Front opening 14"/35.5cm
Length from front opening to back
7"/18cm

Materials
- 2 3½oz/100g skeins (each approx 120yd/110m) of Cascade Yarns *Pacific Chunky* (acrylic/superwash merino wool) in #01 Cream (A) (5)
- 1 skein in #15 Taupe (B)
- One pair each sizes 8 and 11 (5 and 8mm) needles, *or size to obtain gauges*
- Two size 8 (5mm) double-pointed needles (dpn) for I-cord button only
- One pair size 0 (2mm) needles
- Stitch markers

3-Needle Bind-Off
1) Hold right sides of pieces together on two needles. Insert third needle knitwise into first st of each needle and wrap yarn knitwise.
2) Knit these two sts together and slip them off the needles. *Knit the next two sts together in the same manner.
3) Slip first st on 3rd needle over 2nd st and off needle. Rep from * in step 2 across row until all sts are bound off.

Stitch Glossary
K1b Knit 1 in the row below.

Pattern Stitch
(over an even number of sts)
Row 1 (WS) *K1, p1; rep from * to end.
Row 2 (RS) *K1b, p1; rep from * to end.
Rep rows 1 and 2 for pat st.

Front Opening
With size 11 (8mm) needles and A, cast on 66 sts.
Rows 1 and 2 Sl 1, k to last st, p1 tbl.
Row 3 (WS) Sl 1, k to last 3 sts, yo, k2tog, p1 tbl.
Rows 4 and 5 Rep rows 1 and 2.
Row 6 Bind off 22 sts, k to last st, p1 tbl—44 sts.
Change to size 8 (5mm) needles.

BEGIN PATTERN STITCH
Row 1 (WS) Sl 1, k3, *k1, p1; rep from * to last 4 sts, k3, p1 tbl.
Row 2 Sl 1, k3, *k1b, p1; rep from * to last 4 sts, k3, p1 tbl.
Rep rows 1 and 2 for pat st, with 4 garter st edge sts each side, 14 times more, then rep row 1 once more.

Crown Shaping
Row 1 (RS) Sl 1, k3, [k1b, p1] 11 times, k1b, p2tog tbl, turn.
Row 2 Sl 1, [p1, k1] 5 times, p2tog tbl, turn.
Row 3 Sl 1, [p1, k1b] 5 times, p2tog tbl, turn.
Rep rows 2 and 3 ten times more, then rep row 2 once more—20 sts.
Cut yarn, leaving a long tail. Pull tail through center 12 sts and draw up tightly.

Gauges
12 sts and 26 rows to 4"/10cm over pat st using size 8 (5mm) needles.
12 sts and 26 rows to 4"/10cm over garter st using size 11 (8mm) needles. *Take time to check gauges.*

Bear Hat

Using the 3-needle bind-off method, join 4 edge sts each side for center back seam.

Ears (make 2)
With size 8 (5mm) needles and A, cast on 15 sts.

Row 1 (WS) Sl 1, *k1, p1; rep from * to last 2 sts, k1, p1 tbl.

Row 2 Sl 1, *p1, k1b; rep from * to last 2 sts, p1, p1 tbl.

Rows 3–5 Rep rows 1 and 2 once, then rep row 1 once more.

Dec row 6 Sl 1, p1, ssk, *k1b, p1; rep from * to last 5 sts, k1b, k2tog, p1, p1 tbl—13 sts.

Row 7 Sl 1, k1, p2, *k1, p1; rep from * to last 3 sts, p1, k1, p1 tbl.

Dec row 8 Sl 1 , p1, ssk, *p1, k1b; rep from * to last 5 sts, p1, k2tog, p1, p1 tbl—11 sts.

Row 9 Sl 1, *k1, p1; rep from * to last 2 sts, k1, p1 tbl.

Dec rows 10 and 11 Rep rows 6 and 7—9 sts.

Dec row 12 Sl 1, p1, ssk, p1, k2tog, p1, p1 tbl—7 sts.

Row 13 Rep row 9. Bind off.

INNER EAR

With size 8 (5mm) needles, RS facing, and A, pick up and k 20 sts evenly along right shaped side, top, and left shaped side of ear. Change to size 0 (2mm) needles and B.

Row 1 (WS) Sl 1, p to last st, p1 tbl.

Row 2 Sl 1, k to last st, p1 tbl.

Dec row 3 Sl 1, k5, [ssk] twice, [k2tog] twice, k5, p1 tbl—16 sts.

Rows 4, 6, 8, and 10 Rep row 2.

Dec row 5 Sl 1, k3, [ssk] twice, [k2tog] twice, k3, p1 tbl—12 sts.

Dec row 7 Sl 1, k1, [ssk] twice, [k2tog] twice, k1, p1 tbl—8 sts.

Dec row 9 Sl 1, [ssk] 3 times, p1 tbl—5 sts.

Dec row 11 Sl 1, SK2P, p1 tbl—3 sts. Cut yarn, leaving a long tail. Pull tail through rem sts twice, draw up and secure.

I-cord Button
With dpn and B, cast on 4 sts. *Knit one row. Without turning work, slide sts back to the opposite end of needle to work next row from RS. Pull yarn tightly from the end of the row. Rep from * until I-cord measures 5½"/14cm from beg. Bind off, leaving a long tail. Tie a knot in I-cord and sew ends tog to form a triangle-shaped button.

Finishing
Using photo as guide, sew I-cord button to front opening edging and ears on each side of hat. Weave in ends. ∎

11

Cabled Coat

This fashion-forward swing coat features mod shaping, cabled textures, and a sunshiny gradient yarn.

DESIGNED BY CHERYL MURRAY

Sizes

Instructions are written for sizes 2 (4, 6). Shown in size 4.

Knitted Measurements

Chest (closed) 21(23, 25½)"/53 (58.5, 65)cm
Length 16¼ (18¼, 19¼)"/41 (46, 49)cm
Upper arm 8 (8½, 9)"/20.5 (21.5, 23)cm

Materials

■ 3 (3, 4) 3½oz/100g skeins (each approx 213yd/195m) of Cascade Yarns *Pacific Color Wave* (acrylic/superwash merino wool) in #311 Citrus (5)
■ One pair size 7 (4.5mm) needles, *or size to obtain gauge*
■ One size 7 (4.5mm) circular needle, 16"/40cm long
■ Cable needle
■ Stitch holders
■ One 1¼"/33mm button

Stitch Glossary

4-St RC Sl 2 sts to cn and hold to *back*, k2, k2 from cn.
4-St LC Sl 2 sts to cn and hold to *front*, k2, k2 from cn.
6-St RC Sl 3 sts to cn and hold to *back*, k3, k3 from cn.
6-St LC Sl 3 sts to cn and hold to *front*, k3, k3 from cn.

K2, P2 Rib

(over a multiple of 4 sts)
Row 1 (WS) P3, *k2, p2; rep from *, end last rep p3 instead of p2.
Row 2 (RS) K3, *p2, k2; rep from *, end last rep k3 instead of k2.
Rep rows 1 and 2 for k2, p2 rib.

Back

With size 7 (4.5mm) needles, cast on 76 (82, 90) sts.
Set-up row (WS) [P2, k2] 0 (0, 1) times, p0 (3, 3), k2, p2, k2, p4, k2, p2, k2, p10, k2, p2, k2, p4, k4, p4, k2, p2, k2, p10, k2, p2, k2, p4, k2, p2, k2, p0 (3, 3), [k2, p2] 0 (0, 1) times.

BEGIN CHART 1

Inc row (RS) Foll row 1 of chart 1 and beg as indicated for chosen size, work first 19 (22, 26) sts foll chart, M1, k4, M1, work to end of rep line, then work first 16 sts of rep, M1, k4, M1, work to end of rep line, work last 4 (7, 11) sts of chart—80 (86, 94) sts.
Note The inc row is only worked once. Cont to work in pat foll chart rows 2–7 until 20 rows of chart are worked after set-up row.
Dec row (RS) P1 (k1, k1), dec 1 st in pat, work in pat to the last 3 sts, dec 1 st in pat, p1 (k1, k1). Rep dec row every 20th row 3 times more—72 (78, 86) sts.
Work even until piece measures 11 (12½, 13)"/28 (32, 33)cm from beg.

ARMHOLE SHAPING

Cont to work in pat, bind off 6 sts at beg

Gauge

27 sts and 28 rows to 4"/10 cm across chart pats, after blocking, using size 7 (4.5 mm) needles.
Take time to check gauge.

Cabled Coat

of next 2 rows.

Dec row (RS) Work 1 st, dec 1 st in pat, work to last 3 sts, dec 1 st in pat, work 1 st. Rep dec row every other row 3 (5, 7) times more—52 (54, 58) sts. Work even until armhole measures 4½ (5, 5½)"/11.5 (12.5, 14)cm. On the last WS row, pm to mark the center 34 sts.

NECK AND SHOULDER SHAPING
Next row (RS) Bind off 3 sts, work to the center marked sts, join a 2nd ball of yarn and bind off 34 sts, work to end. Bind off 3 sts at beg of next WS row, then cont to shape shoulders by binding off 3 (3, 4) sts from each shoulder edge once, then 2 (3, 4) sts once and, AT THE SAME TIME, dec 1 st from each neck edge on the next RS row.

Pocket Linings (make 2)
Cast on 20 sts. Work in St st (k on RS, p on WS) for 4½"/11.5 cm. Sl sts to holder.

Left Front
With size 7 (4.5 mm) needles, cast on 39 (42, 46) sts.
Set-up row (WS) P1, k2, p4, k2, p2, k2, p10, k2, p2, k2, p4, k2, p2, k2, p0 (3, 3), k0 (0, 2), p0 (0, 2).

BEGIN CHART 1
Inc row 1 (RS) Foll row 1 of chart and beg as indicated for chosen size, work first 19 (22, 26) sts foll chart, M1, k4, M1, work to end of rep line, k1—41 (44, 48) sts.
Note The inc row is only worked once. Cont to work in pat foll chart rep rows 2–7 until 20 rows of chart are worked after set-up row.
Dec row (RS) P1 (k1, k1), dec 1 st in pat, work to end of row.
Rep dec row every 20th row 3 times

more and, AT THE SAME TIME, when piece measures 7"/18 cm from beg, on next RS row work the pocket lining placement as foll:
Pocket row (RS) Work to the last 29 sts, sl the next 20 sts to a st holder and, working across the lining sts from holder, k2, p2, k12, p2, k2, then work rem 9 sts in pat. Cont to work the left front, cont decs as established. When all 4 dec rows are completed, work even on rem 37 (40, 44) sts until piece measures same as back to armhole, end with a WS row.

ARMHOLE SHAPING
Next row (RS) Bind off 6 sts, work to end. Work 1 row even.
Dec row (RS) Work 1 st, dec 1 st in pat, work to end.
Rep dec row every other row 3 (5, 7) times more—27 (28, 30) sts.
Work even until armhole measures 2½

(3, 3½)"/6.5 (7.5, 9)cm, end with a RS row.

NECK SHAPING
Next row (WS) Bind off 13 sts (neck edge), work to end.
Cont to shape neck by binding off 2 sts from neck edge once, then dec 1 st every RS row 4 times—8 (9, 11) sts.
Work even until armhole measures 4½ (5, 5½)"/11.5 (12.5, 14)cm.

SHOULDER SHAPING
Bind off 3 sts from shoulder edge once, 3 (3, 4) sts once, and 2 (3, 4) sts once.

Right Front
Cast on 39 (42, 46) sts.
Set-up row (WS) [P2, k2] 0 (0, 1) times, p0 (3, 3), k2, p2, k2, p4, k2, p2, k2, p10, k2, p2, k2, p4, k2, p1.

BEGIN CHART 1
Inc row 1 (RS) Foll row 1 of chart beg at RF. Work first 16 sts of chart, M1, k4, M1, work to end of chart for chosen size.
Note The inc row is worked only once. Cont to work in pat foll chart rep rows 2–7 until 20 rows of chart are worked after set-up row.
Dec row (RS) Work to last 3 sts, dec 1 st in pat, work 1 st. Rep dec row every 20th row 3 times more and, AT THE SAME TIME, when piece measures 7"/18cm from beg, on next RS row work the pocket lining placement as foll:
Pocket row (RS) Work 9 sts as established, sl the next 20 sts to a st holder, working across the lining sts from holder, k2, p2, k12, p2, k2, then work rem sts in pat as established. Cont to work to correspond to left front, reversing all shaping.

Sleeves
With size 7 (4.5 mm) needles, cast on 50 sts.

Cabled Coat

Set-up row (WS) P4, k2, p2, k2, p4, k2, p2, k2, p10, k2, p2, k2, p4, k2, p2, k2, p4.

BEGIN CHART 2
Inc row 1 (RS) Foll row 1 of chart 2 and beg with the first st, work 23 sts foll chart, M1, k4, M1, work rem 23 sts foll chart—52 sts.
Note The inc row is worked only once. Cont to foll chart 2, rep rows 2–7 and, AT THE SAME TIME, inc 1 st (working incs into k2, p2 rib) each side every 6th row 0 (0, 5) times, then every 8th row 1 (2, 0) times, then every 10th row 0 (1, 0) times—54 (58, 62) sts.
Work even until piece measures 4½"/11.5cm from beg.

CAP SHAPING
Bind off 6 sts at beg of next 2 rows. Dec 1 st each side of next RS row, then every other row 3 (5, 7) times more. Dec 1 st each side *every* row 3 times. Dec 1 st each side every other row 4 times. Bind off 2 sts at beg of next 2 rows.

Bind off 3 sts at beg of next 2 rows. Bind off rem 10 sts.

Finishing
Block pieces to measurements. Sew shoulder seams. Set in sleeves. Sew side and sleeve seams.

POCKET TRIMS
Sl 20 sts from pocket holder to needle. Rejoin yarn from the RS.
Row 1 (RS) K2, p2, k2, p2tog, p1, k2, p1, p2tog, k2, p2, k2—18 sts. Work 3 rows more in k2, p2 rib. Bind off in rib. Sew side of the trim in place to the front. Sew the pocket linings in place on the WS.

FRONT TRIM
From the RS, pick up and k 76 (84, 88) sts along center right front edge. Beg with a WS row, work in k2, p2 rib for 10 rows. Bind off in rib. Rep on center left front edge.

NECKBAND
With RS facing and circular needle, pick up and k 39 sts from right front neck edge, 34 sts from back neck edge, and 39 sts from left front neck edge—112 sts. Work in k2, p2 rib for 4 rows.
Buttonhole row (WS) Work in rib to the last 10 sts, bind off 5 sts, work to end. On next row, cast on 5 sts over the bound-off sts. Work 4 rows more in k2, p2 rib. Bind off in rib.
Sew button opposite buttonhole. ∎

STITCH KEY

☐	k on RS, p on WS
⊟	p on RS, k on WS
M	M1
	4-st RC
	4-st LC
	6-st RC
	6-st LC

CHART 2

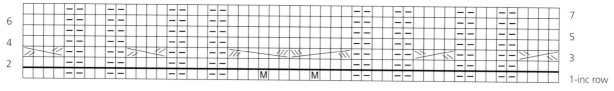

52 sts

CHART 1

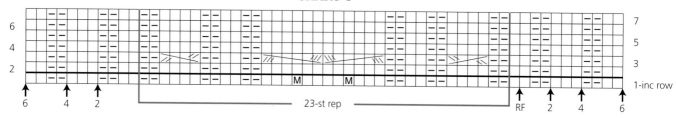

23-st rep

5½"   1 (1¼, 1½)"

¾ "

BACK

4½ (5, 5½)"

16¼ (18¼, 19¼)"

11 (12½, 13)"

12 (12¾, 14)"

10½ (11½, 12¾)"

1 (1¼, 1½)"

¾ "

LEFT
FRONT

4½ (5, 5½)"

13 (14½, 15)"

11 (12½, 13)"

6 (6½, 7)"

5½ (6, 6½)"

8 (8½, 9)"

3½ (4, 4½)"

SLEEVE

4½"

7¾ "

Pinwheel Lace Tunic

Pretty pinwheels dance down the front of this sweet tunic,
as little scallops line up across the hem.

DESIGNED BY DIANE ZANGL

Sizes
Instructions are written for sizes 4 (6).
Shown in size 4.

Knitted Measurements
Chest 25 (27½)"/63.5 (70)cm
Length 19½ (21)"/49.5 (53.5)cm
Upper arm 10½ (11½)"/26.5 (29)cm

Materials
- 3 3½oz/100g skeins (each approx 213yd/195m) of Cascade Yarns *Pacific* (acrylic/superwash merino wool) in #26 Lavender 〔4〕
- One size 6 (4mm) circular needle, 24"/60cm long, *or size to obtain gauge*
- One pair size 6 (4mm) needles
- Size G/6 (4mm) crochet hook
- Stitch markers
- One ½"/12mm button

Notes
1) Body is worked in one piece to the underarms.
2) Chart is worked in the round up to the underarms, then worked back and forth.

Stitch Glossary
GS (gathering st) Sl next st off LH needle and unravel it all the way down, including cast-on st. You will have 7

"ladder rungs." Insert RH needle under all rungs, pull up a long st and place on LH needle. Knit this st.

Scalloped Edge
(over a multiple of 6 sts)
Rnd 1 Purl.
Rnds 2–5 Knit.
Rnd 6 (scallop rnd) K3, *GS, k5; rep from * around, end last rep k2.
Work rnds 1–6 for scalloped edge.

Body
With circular needle, cast on 144 (156) sts. Join, taking care not to twist sts, and pm for beg of rnd.
Work rnds 1–6 of scalloped edge.
Next rnd K72 (78), pm (side marker), k to end.
Work even in St st (k every rnd) for 0 (2) rnds.

BEGIN CHART PATTERN
Next rnd K23 (26), pm (chart marker), work rnd 1 of chart over next 26 sts, pm (chart marker), k to end. Keeping 26 sts between chart markers in chart pat and rem sts in St st, work chart through rnd 30 (32), then rep rnds 1–30 (1–32) for chart pat.
AT THE SAME TIME, work even until piece measures 4½ (5)"/11.5 (12.5)cm from beg.
Dec rnd K2tog, k to 2 sts before side marker, ssk, sm, k2tog, k to 2 sts before end of rnd marker, ssk, sm—4 sts dec'd.
Rep dec rnd every 25 rnds twice more—132 (144) sts.
Work even until piece measures 14½ (15½)"/37 (39.5)cm from beg, end last even-numbered rnd at 3 sts before end of rnd.

DIVIDE FOR FRONT AND BACK
Next rnd Bind off 6 sts, dropping end-of-rnd marker (left armhole), work

Gauge
21 sts and 28 rnds to 4"/10cm over St st using size 6 (4mm) needles.
Take time to check gauge.

Pinwheel Lace Tunic

in pat as established to 3 sts before side marker, bind off next 6 sts, dropping side marker (right armhole), leave 60 (66) sts just worked on needle for front (make note of last rnd worked), change to straight needles and knit to end for back—60 (66) back sts.

Back
Next row (WS) Purl.
Cont to work back and forth in St st (k on RS, p on WS) as foll:

ARMHOLE SHAPING
Dec 1 st each side on next row, then *every* row twice more—54 (60) sts. Work even until armhole measures 2 (2½)"/5 (6.5)cm, end with a WS row.

DIVIDE FOR BACK NECK OPENING
Next row (RS) K27 (30), join a 2nd ball of yarn and k27 (30). Working both sides at once with separate balls of yarn, work even until armhole measures 4½ (5)"/11.5 (12.5)cm, end with a WS row.

NECK SHAPING
Next row (RS) With first ball of yarn, k to end; with 2nd ball of yarn, bind off 10 (11) sts, k to end.
Next row (WS) With 2nd ball of yarn, p to end; with first ball of yarn, bind off 10 (11) sts, purl to end.
Dec 1 st from each neck edge on next row, then *every* row twice more—14 (16) sts each side.
Work even until armhole measures 5 (5½)"/12.5 (14)cm, end with a WS row. Bind off sts each side for shoulders.

Front
With WS facing, work back and forth as foll:
Next row (WS) Purl. Cont to work chart, working odd rows (RS rows) foll chart and even rows (WS rows) in purl.
AT THE SAME TIME, shape armhole as foll:

ARMHOLE SHAPING
Dec 1 st each side on next row, then *every* row twice more—54 (60) sts. Work even until armhole measures 3 (3½)"/7.5 (9)cm, end with a WS row, AT THE SAME TIME, when 4 chart reps have been completed, work all sts in St st, dropping chart markers.

NECK SHAPING
Next row (RS) K17 (19), join a 2nd ball of yarn, bind off center 20 (22) sts, k to end. Working both sides at once, dec 1 st from each neck edge on next row, then *every* row twice more—14 (16) sts each side. Work even until same length as back to shoulder. Bind off sts each side.

Sleeves
With straight needles, cast on 49 (54) sts. Work in St st, inc 1 st each side on first row, then every row 4th row twice more—55 (60) sts. Work even until piece measures 2½"/6.5cm from beg, end with a WS row. Mark beg and end of last row for beg of cap.

CAP SHAPING
Work even for ½"/1.5cm, end with a WS row. Dec 1 st each side on next row, then every row twice more—49 (54) sts. Bind off.

Finishing
Block pieces to measurements. Sew shoulder and sleeve seams. Set in sleeves.

Chart row numbers (right side, odd rows shown): 31, 32, 29, 27, 25, 23, 21, 19, 17, 15, 13, 11, 9, 7, 5, 3, 1

26 sts

STITCH KEY
- ☐ k when working in rnds, p on WS when working back and forth
- ⟋ k2tog
- ⟍ ssk
- ⟋ k3tog
- ◯ yo

NECK EDGING

With crochet hook and RS facing, join yarn with a sl st at base of back neck opening.
Rnd 1 Making sure that work lies flat, sc around entire neck, working 2 sc in each corner of back neck. Join rnd with a sl st in first st.
Rnd 2 (button loop) Ch 1, working from left to right, sc in each st to top corner of right back opening, ch 5 for button loop, sl st in next st, cont working from left to right, sc in each rem st around. Join rnd with a sl st in first st. Fasten off.

SLEEVE EDGING

With crochet hook and RS facing, join yarn with a sl st in underarm seam.
Rnd 1 Making sure that work lies flat, sc around entire edge. Join rnd with a sl st in first st.
Rnd 2 Ch 1, working from left to right, sc in each st around. Join rnd with a sl st in first st. Fasten off. Sew button to top corner of left back opening. ■

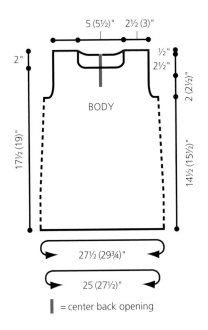

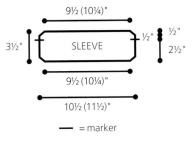

Garter Cardi

Say hello to cozy pockets and comfy style!
Speedy garter stitch and a chunky gauge make this cardi a quick-knit classic.

DESIGNED BY AUDREY DRYSDALE

Sizes
Instructions are written for sizes 2 (4, 6).
Shown in size 4.

Knitted Measurements
Chest (closed) 26(28, 31)"/66 (71, 78.5)cm
Length 13½ (14, 15)"/34 (35.5, 38)cm
Upper arm 9¼ (10, 11)"/23.5 (25.5, 28)cm

Materials
■ 4 (5, 5) 3½oz/100g skeins (each
approx 120yd/110m) of Cascade Yarns
Pacific Chunky (acrylic/superwash merino
wool) in #95 Lime Green ⑤
■ One pair each sizes 8 and 10 (5 and
6mm) needles, *or size to obtain gauge*
■ Stitch holders
■ Removable stitch markers
■ Five ¹¹⁄₁₆"/18mm buttons

K1, P1 Rib
(over an odd number of sts)
Row 1 (RS) K1, *p1, k1; rep from * to end.
Row 2 P1, *k1, p1; rep from * to end.
Rep rows 1 and 2 for k1, p1 rib.

Back
With smaller needles, cast on 43 (47, 51)
sts. Work in k1, p1 rib for 4 rows, dec 1
st at center of the last WS row—42 (46,

50) sts. Change to larger needles.
Work in garter st (k every row) until piece
measures 8½ (8½, 9)"/21.5 (21.5, 23)cm
from beg.

RAGLAN ARMHOLE SHAPING
Bind off 2 sts at beg of next 2 rows.
Dec row (RS) K2, k2tog, k to last 4 sts,
ssk, k2—2 sts dec'd.
Rep dec row every 4th row once more,
then every other row 10 (11, 13) times
more—14 (16, 16) sts. Sl these sts to a st
holder.

Left Front
With smaller needles, cast on 21 (23, 25)
sts. Work in k1, p1 rib for 4 rows.
Change to larger needles.
Work in garter st until piece measures
8½ (8½, 9)"/21.5 (21.5, 23)cm from beg.

RAGLAN ARMHOLE SHAPING
Bind off 2 sts at beg of next RS row,
k to end. Knit 1 row.
Dec row (RS) K2, k2tog, k to end—1 st
dec'd.
Rep dec row every 4th row once more,
then every other row 5 (6, 8) times—12
(13, 13) sts. Knit 1 row.

NECK SHAPING
Next row (RS) K2, k2tog, k5 (6, 6), turn.
Sl the rem 3 sts to holder.
Knit 1 row.
Dec row K2, k2tog, k to last 2 sts,
k2tog.
Rep the last 2 rows 1 (2, 2) times
more—4 (3, 3) sts.
Knit 1 row.
Next row K2 (1, 1), k2tog.
Next row K3 (2, 2).

For size 2 only
Next row K1, k2tog.
For all sizes
Next row K2tog. Fasten off last st.

POCKET
In the first garter ridge row at lower
edge, mark the 4th st from the side seam
with a removable stitch marker. From the
RS, using larger needles, beg in this first
marked st, pick up and k 18 (20, 22) sts
to center edge.
Knit 5 rows.
Dec row (RS) K2, k2tog, k to end.
Next row Knit.
Rep the last 2 rows 8 (9, 9) times
more—9 (10, 12) sts. Bind off knitwise on
the WS row. Sew side and top edge of

Gauge
13 sts and 26 rows to 4"/10cm over garter st using larger needles.
Take time to check gauge.

Garter Cardi

pocket to sweater front front. Use removable stitch markers to hold the pocket and front tog at center edge.

Right Front

Work same as left front to the raglan armhole shaping, ending with a RS row.

RAGLAN ARMHOLE SHAPING

Bind off 2 sts at beg of next WS row.
Dec row (RS) K to last 4 sts, ssk, k2—1 st dec'd.
Rep dec row every 4th row once more, then every other row 5 (6, 8) times more—12 (13, 13) sts.
Knit 1 row.

NECK SHAPING

Next row (RS) Sl first 3 sts to holder, rejoin yarn and k to last 4 sts, ssk, k2—8 (9, 9) sts.
Knit 1 row.
Dec row K2tog, k to last 4 sts, ssk, k2.
Rep the last 2 rows 1 (2, 2) times more—4 (3, 3) sts.
Knit 1 row.
Next row Ssk, k2 (1, 1).
Next row K3 (2, 2).

For size 2 only
Next row K2tog, k1.
Next row K2.
For all sizes
Next row Ssk. Fasten off last st.

POCKET

In the first garter ridge row at lower edge, mark the 4th st from the side seam with a removeable stitch marker.

From the RS, using larger needles, beg at center edge, pick up and k 18 (20, 22) sts to the marker.
Knit 5 rows.
Dec row (RS) K to last 4 sts, ssk, k2.
Next row Knit.
Rep the last 2 rows 8 (9, 9) times more—9 (10, 12) sts. Bind off knitwise on the WS row. Complete same as left front pocket.

Sleeves

With smaller needles, cast on 23 (25, 29) sts. Work in k1, p1 rib for 4 rows, inc 1 st at center on the last WS row—24 (26, 30) sts. Change to larger needles.
Work in garter st for 4 rows.
Inc 1 st each side of next row then every 12th row twice more—30 (32, 36) sts.
Work even until piece measures 6½ (8½, 9½)"/16.5 (21.5, 24) cm from beg.
Note This sleeve length is for a 3/4-length sleeve, as seen in photo. Add 2"/5cm to the length if a traditional sleeve length is desired.

RAGLAN CAP SHAPING

Bind off 2 sts at beg of next 2 rows.
Dec row (RS) K2, k2tog, k to last 4 sts, ssk, k2—2 sts dec'd.
Rep dec row every 4th row 4 times more, then every other row 4 (5, 7) times—8 sts. Sl these 8 sts to a st holder.

Finishing

Block pieces to measurements.
Sew raglan sleeve caps into raglan armholes.

NECKBAND

With RS facing and smaller needles, k3 from the right front st holder, pick up and k 7 sts from the shaped front neck edge, k8 from the right sleeve st holder, dec 2 sts across these sleeve sts, k14 (16, 16) from back neck holder, dec 1 st at center of these back neck sts, k8 from the left sleeve st holder, dec 2 sts across these sleeve sts, pick up and k 7 sts from shaped front neck, k3 from the left front st holder—45 (47, 47) sts.
Beg with pat row 2, work in k1, p1 rib for 5 rows. Bind off in rib.

BUTTON BAND

With RS facing and smaller needles, pick up and k 53 (54, 58) sts evenly along straight left front edge, picking up through both fabric thicknesses along the pocket edge. Knit 4 rows.
Bind off knitwise.

BUTTONHOLE BAND

Pick up and k 53 (54, 58) sts along straight right front edge same as button band. Knit 1 row.

Buttonhole row (RS) K3 (2, 2), [k2tog, yo, k9 (10, 11)] 4 times, k2tog, yo, k4 (2, 2).
Knit 2 rows more. Bind off knitwise.
Sew buttons opposite buttonholes. ■

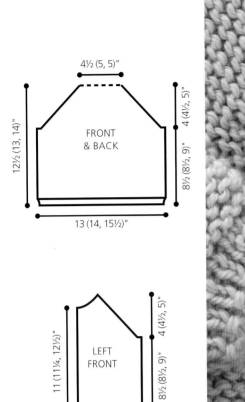

4½ (5, 5)"

12½ (13, 14)"

FRONT & BACK

4 (4½, 5)"

8½ (8½, 9)"

13 (14, 15½)"

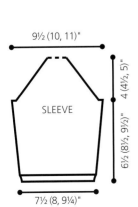

4 (4½, 5)"

11 (11¼, 12½)"

LEFT FRONT

8½ (8½, 9)"

6½ (7, 7½)"

9½ (10, 11)"

4 (4½, 5)"

SLEEVE

6½ (8½, 9½)"

7½ (8, 9¼)"

Playtime Henley

Knit in the round with fat tonal stripes, this easy top-down raglan is a durable sweater for playtime fun.

DESIGNED BY STACEY GERBMAN

Sizes
Instructions are written for sizes 12–18 months (2, 3, 4, 5). Shown in size 3.

Knitted Measurements
Chest 20¼ (22, 23½, 25, 27)"/51.5 (56, 50, 63.5, 68.5)cm
Length 12 (12¾, 13½, 14¼, 15)"/30.5 (32.5, 34.5, 37, 38)cm
Upper arm 7¼ (7¼, 8¾, 8¾, 9¼)"/18.5 (18.5, 22, 22, 23.5)cm

Materials
- 1 3½oz/100g skein (each approx 213yds/195m) each of Cascade Yarns *Pacific* (acrylic/superwash merino wool) in #02 White (A), #06 Baby Pink (B), #18 Cotton Candy (C), and #106 Carmine Rose (D) (4)
- Two size 6 (4mm) circular needles, one 16"/40cm and one 24"/60cm long, *or size to obtain gauge*
- One size 7 (4.5mm) circular needle, 24"/60cm long
- One set (5) each sizes 6 and 7 (4 and 4.5mm) double-pointed needles (dpn)
- 3 (3, 3, 4, 4) 1"/2.5cm buttons
- Tapestry needle
- Stitch markers
- Stitch holder

Note
Sweater is worked from the top down in rows from cast on to the end of the raglan increases, then joined to work in the round.

Stitch Glossary
M1R (make 1 right) Insert LH needle from *back to front* into horizontal strand between last st worked and next st on LH needle. Knit through front loop to twist st.

M1L (make 1 left) Insert LH needle from *front to back* into horizontal strand between last st worked and next st on LH needle. Knit through back loop to twist st.

Yoke
With A and smaller, shorter circular needle, cast on 58 (62, 66, 70, 74) sts for the neck.

Row 1 (RS) *K2, p2; rep from *, end k2.
Row 2 (WS) *P2, k2; rep from *, end p2.
Rows 3–6 Rep rows 1 and 2 twice more.
Row 7 Rep row 1.
Change to larger circular needle.
Row 8 (WS) P11 (12, 12, 13, 13) for right front, pm, p1, k2 (2, 3, 3, 4), M1, k2 (2, 3, 3, 4), p1 for right sleeve, pm, p1, k22 (24, 24, 26, 26), p1 for back, pm, p1, k2 (2, 3, 3, 4), M1, k2 (2, 3, 3, 4), p1 for left sleeve, pm, p11 (12, 12, 13, 13) for left front—60 (64, 68, 72, 76) sts total.

Gauge
20 sts and 28 rows to 4"/10cm over St st using larger needles.
Take time to check gauge.

Playtime Henley

RAGLAN SHAPING

Inc row 1 (RS) K to 1 st before marker, M1R, k1, sm, k1, M1L, *p to 1 st before next marker, M1R, k1, sm, k1, M1L, rep from * twice more, k to end of row—8 sts inc'd.

Row 2 (WS) P to marker, sm, p1, *k to 1 st before next marker, p1, sm, p1, rep from * twice more, p to end.

Rep rows 1 and 2 for 5 (5, 6, 6, 7) times more.

Change to B and rep rows 1 and 2 for 5 (6, 6, 7, 7) times more—148 (160, 172, 184, 196) sts.

Place all sts on holder, removing markers.

BUTTONHOLE PLACKET

With RS facing and A, beg at lower edge, pick up and k 26 (30, 30, 34, 34) sts along left front placket edge, ending at top of ribbed neckband.

Row 1 (WS) *K2, p2; rep from *, end k2.

Row 2 *P2, k2; rep from *, end p2.

Buttonhole Row 3 [K2, p2, k2, yo, p2tog] 3 (3, 3, 4, 4) times, k2, p0 (2, 2, 0, 0), k0 (2, 2, 0, 0).

Row 4 Rep row 2.

Rows 5 and 6 Rep rows 1 and 2 once more. Bind off all sts in pat.

BUTTON PLACKET

With RS facing and A, beg at top of neck edge, pick up and k 26 (30, 30, 34, 34) sts along right front placket edge, ending at lower edge.

Rep rows 1 and 2 of buttonhole placket 3 times.

Bind off all sts in pat.

JOIN BODY IN THE ROUND

Transfer sts from st holder to larger circular needle ready to work a RS row. Transfer the last 23 (25, 26, 28, 29) sts from RH needle to LH needle.

Joining rnd With B, k23 (25, 26, 28, 29) sts before placket, overlap placket bands with buttonhole band on top of button band and, working through both placket bands, pick up and k 4 sts along sides of band, k23 (25, 26, 28, 29), place next 29 (31, 35, 37, 41) sts on st holder for left sleeve, cast on 2 (2, 3, 3, 4) sts, pm for side, cast on 2 (2, 3, 3, 4) sts, p44 (48, 50, 54, 56), place next 29 (31, 35, 37, 41) sts on st holder for right sleeve, cast on 2 (2, 3, 3, 4) sts, pm for side, cast on 2 (2, 3, 3, 4) sts. The 2nd marker now marks beg of rnd—102 (110, 118, 126, 134) sts.

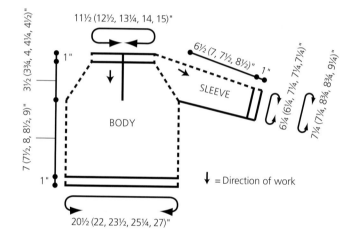

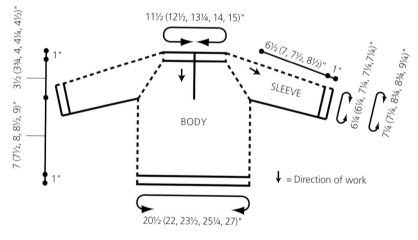

Body

Rnd 1 With B, k54 (58, 62, 66, 70), sm, p to end of rnd.

Rnds 2–3 Rep rnd 1.

Rnd 4 P1, k to 1 st before marker, p1, sm, p to end of rnd.

Rnd 5 P the purl sts and k the knit sts.

Rnd 6 P2, k to 2 sts before marker, p2, sm, p to end of rnd.

Rnd 7 Rep rnd 5.

Cont in this manner, purling one additional st after beg-of-rnd marker and before 2nd marker every other rnd, and purling all back sts, AT THE SAME TIME, work until there are a total of 20 (22, 22, 24, 26) B rnds.

Change to C and work another 20 (22, 22, 24, 26) rnds.

Change to D and work until body measures 7 (7½, 8, 8½, 9)"/18 (10, 20.5, 21.5, 23)cm from joining rnd.

Change to smaller, longer needle and work 1 rnd, inc 2 sts evenly around—104 (112, 120, 128, 136) sts.

Rnds 1–7 *K2, p2; rep from * around.
Bind off all sts loosely in pat.

Sleeves

Transfer 29 (31, 35, 37, 41) sts from holder and divide sts evenly over 4 larger dpn. With B, pick up and k 7 (5, 9, 7, 5) sts at underarm, pm in center of picked up sts to mark beg of rnd, and join—36 (36, 44, 44, 46) sts.

Turn sweater WS out, to work sleeves from the WS.

Work in St st (k every rnd) for 1"/2.5cm, then dec as follows:

Dec rnd K2tog, k to last 2 sts, ssk—2 sts dec'd.

Change to C and cont in St st, rep dec

row every 6th rnd 1 (1, 3, 3, 4) times more—32 (32, 36, 36, 36) sts.

Cont in St st until there are 20 (22, 22, 24, 24) rnds in C.

Change to D and cont in St st until sleeve measures 6½ (7, 7½, 8 , 8½)"/16.5 (18, 19, 20.5, 21.5)cm from underarm.

Change to smaller dpn and work in k2, p2 rib for 5 rnds. Bind off in pat.

Finishing

Turn sweater RS out so sleeves show reverse St st side.

Weave in ends and block sweater to measurements.

Sew buttons opposite buttonholes. ■

15 Striped Wristers

Paired with t-shirts or tutus, these easy-to-knit wristers
will be a favorite among kids of all stripes.

DESIGNED BY MATTHEW SCHRANK

■□□▭

Knitted Measurements
Length 4"/10cm
Circumference (unstretched) 6¼"/16cm

Materials
■ 1 3½oz/100g skein (each 120yds/110m)
of Cascade Yarns *Pacific Chunky* (acrylic/
superwash merino wool) each in #94 Jet
Heather (A) and #62 Charcoal (B) (**5**)
■ One pair each sizes 9 and 10 (5.5 and
6mm) needles, *or size to obtain gauge*

Note
These wristers can easily be made into
fingerless gloves by leaving a hole for the
thumb when seaming the sides.

Wristers
With smaller needles and A, cast on 22 sts.
Row 1 (WS) K3, [p2, k2] 4 times, p3.
Rows 3–9 K the knit sts and p the purl
sts for k2, p2 rib.
Change to larger needles.
Row 10 (RS) With B, knit.
Row 11 (WS) With B, purl.
Row 12 With A, knit.
Row 13 With A, purl.
Repeat rows 10–13 once more, then
repeat rows 10 and 11 once more.
Cut B. Change to smaller needles.
Row 20 With A, knit.
Row 21 Repeat row 1.
Rows 22 and 23 K the knit sts and p the
purl sts for k2, p2 rib.
Bind off in pat on WS.

Finishing
Weave in ends and block pieces to
measurements.
Line up stripes and seam edges. ■

Gauge
14 sts and 20 rows to 4"/10cm over St st using larger needles. *Take time to check gauge.*

16 Striped Scarf

Worked in sporty stripes, this reversible retro scarf will keep kiddos warm on the field and off.

DESIGNED BY ANN FAITH

Knitted Measurements
Width 4"/10cm
Length 38"/96.5cm

Materials
- 1 3½oz/100g skein (each approx 213yd/195m) of Cascade Yarns *Pacific* (acrylic/superwash merino wool) each in #53 Beet (A), #84 Persimmon (B), #01 Cream (C), and #36 Christmas Red (D) 🄸
- One set size 8 (5mm) needles, *or size to obtain gauge*
- Size H/8 (5mm) crochet hook
- Scrap yarn for provisional cast-on
- Stitch marker

Provisional Cast-On
Using scrap yarn and crochet hook, chain the number of sts to cast on, plus a few extra. Cut a tail and pull the tail through the last chain. With knitting needle and working yarn, pick up and knit the stated number of sts through the purl bumps on the back of the chain. To remove scrap-yarn chain, when instructed, pull out the tail from the last crochet st. Gently and slowly pull on the tail to unravel the crochet sts, carefully placing each released knit st on a needle

Note
Scarf begins with a provisional cast-on.

The first section is worked in garter st (k every row) stripes to the first point. The 2nd section is picked up along the cast-on edge and work in the opposite direction in garter st stripes to the 2nd point.

Scarf
FIRST SECTION
With A and using provisional cast-on, cast on 18 sts.
Rows 1–10 With A, knit
Rows 11–20 With B, knit
Rows 21–30 With A, knit.

Rows 31–34 With C, knit.
Rows 35–36 With D, knit.
Rows 37–40 With C, knit.
Repeat rows 1–40 three times more.
Next 2 rows With A, knit.
With A, cont in garter st while binding off 2 sts at beg of next 8 rows—2 sts rem. K last 2 sts and pull yarn through, leaving tail to attach tassel.

SECOND SECTION
Carefully remove scrap yarn from provisional cast-on and place live sts on needle.
Rows 1–4 With C, knit.
Rows 5–6 With D, knit.
Rows 7–10 With C, knit.
Rows 11–20 With A, knit.
Rows 21–30 With B, knit.
Rows 31–40 With A, knit.
Repeat rows 1–40 twice more.
Repeat rows 1–10 once more.
Next 2 rows With A, knit.
With A, cont in garter st while binding off 2 sts at beg of next 8 rows—2 sts rem. K last 2 sts and pull yarn through, leaving tail to attach tassel.

Finishing
Weave in ends and block scarf gently. Make and attach tassels ∎

Gauge
18 sts and 34 rows to 4"/10cm over garter st using size 8 (5mm) needles. *Take time to check gauge.*

Clown Mittens

Clown around in these fun colorwork mittens!
They're worked flat using the intarsia method, then seamed.

DESIGNED BY ANN FAITH

Sizes
Instructions are written for sizes 2 (4–6).
Shown in size 2.

Knitted Measurements
Hand circumference 5½ (6½)"/14 (16.5)cm
Length 6 (7)"/15 (18)cm

Materials
■ 1 3½oz/100g skein (each approx
213yd/195m) of Cascade Yarns *Pacific*
(acrylic/superwash merino wool) each in
#53 Beet (A), #84 Persimmon (B),
#01 Cream (C), #36 Christmas Red (D),
and #46 Lapis (E) (4)
■ One pair size 8 (5mm) needles,
or size to obtain gauge
■ Stitch markers
■ Stitch holder

Note
Chart is worked in St st. When changing
colors, twist yarns on WS to prevent
holes in work. Carry color not in use
loosely across back of work to avoid
puckering. For longer floats, twist carried
and working yarns every few sts.

Right Mitten
With A, cast on 26 (30) sts.
Row 1 (RS) *K2, p2; rep from *, end k2.
Row 2 *P2, k2; rep from *, end p2.
Rep last 2 rows for k2, p2 rib until piece
measures 1½ (2)"/4 (5)cm from beg, end
with a WS row.
Work in St st (k on RS, p on WS) for 4
rows. Cut A.

SHAPE THUMB GUSSET
Join B and cont in St st, working thumb
gusset as foll:
Inc row (RS) K12 (14), pm, [kfb] twice,
pm, k12 (14)—28 (32) sts.
Next row Purl.
Inc row K to next marker, sm, kfb,
k to 1 st before next marker, kfb, sm,
k to end—30 (34) sts.
Next row Purl.

BEGIN CHART
Inc row (RS) With B, k0 (2), pm, work
next 10 sts foll row 1 of chart, with B
k to next marker, sm, kfb, k to 1 st before
next marker, kfb, sm, with B k to end—
32 (36) sts.
Next row Purl.
Rep last two rows twice more—12 sts
between thumb markers.
Next row (RS) Cont in pat to next
thumb marker, remove marker, k12
thumb sts then sl them to a st holder,
cast on 2 sts with B, remove marker, k to
end—26 (30) sts.
Cont in St st and chart pat until 14 rows
of chart are complete, then work 1 (3)
rows with B over all sts. Cut B.

Gauge
18 sts and 24 rows to 4"/10cm over St st using size 8 (5mm) needles.
Take time to check gauge.

Clown Mittens

SHAPE TOP
Row 1 (WS) Join A and purl.
Dec row 2 K3, [k2tog, k3 (1)] 4 (8) times, k3—22 sts.
Row 3 Join D and purl.
Dec row 4 K2, [k2tog, k1] 6 times, k2—16 sts.
Row 5 With A, purl.
Dec row 6 [K2tog] 8 times—8 sts.
Row 7 With D, purl.
Dec row 8 [K2tog] 4 times.
Cut yarn and pull through rem 4 sts.

FACE
Refer to chart for placement. Embroider mouth with D, using duplicate st. Embroider eyes with E, using duplicate st.

THUMB
Place 12 thumb sts on needle. With WS facing, join A. Work 4 (6) rows in St st, end with a RS row.
Dec row (WS) [P2tog] 6 times—6 sts.
Dec row [K2tog] 3 times.
Cut yarn, leaving an end for sewing, and pull through rem 3 sts.

Left Mitten
Work same as right mitten, reversing chart placement as foll:

BEGIN CHART
Next row (RS) With B, k to 0 (2) sts after 2nd thumb marker, pm, work next 10 sts foll row 1 of chart, k to end with B.
Next row Purl.
Complete same as right mitten.

Finishing
Weave in ends and block to measurements. Sew side and thumb seams. ■

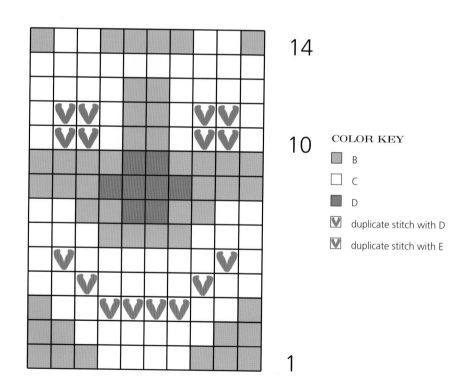

14

10

1

COLOR KEY
☐ B
☐ C
☐ D
Ⅴ duplicate stitch with D
Ⅴ duplicate stitch with E

Simple Cardi

This everyday cardigan goes with everything, knits up quickly, and is a perfect first sweater project for a beginning knitter.

DESIGNED BY YOKO HATTA

Sizes
Instructions are written for sizes 2 (4, 6). Shown in size 2.

Knitted Measurements
Chest (closed) 25½ (27½, 29½)"/64.5 (70, 75)cm
Length 13¼ (14¼, 15¼)"/33.5 (36, 39)cm
Upper arm 11 (12, 13)"/28 (30.5, 33)cm

Materials
■ 2 (2, 3) 3½oz/100g skeins (each approx 213yd/195m) of Cascade Yarns *Pacific* (acrylic/superwash merino wool) in #21 Turquoise ④
■ One pair each sizes 4 and 6 (3.5 and 4mm) needles, *or size to obtain gauge*
■ Stitch holders
■ Six ⅝"/15mm buttons

3-Needle Bind-Off
1) Hold right sides of pieces together on two needles. Insert third needle knitwise into first st on each needle and wrap yarn knitwise.
2) Knit these two sts together and drop them from the needles. *Knit the next two sts together in the same manner.
3) Pass first st on third needle over second st and off needle. Rep from * in step 2 across row until all sts are bound off.

Garter Stitch
Knit every row.

Reverse Stockinette Stitch
Purl on RS rows; knit on WS rows.

Body
With smaller needles, cast on 126 (136, 146) sts. Knit 7 rows. Change to larger needles. Beg with a WS (or knit) row, work in reverse St st until piece measures 7¾ (8¼, 8¾)"/19.5 (21, 22.5)cm from beg, end with a RS (or purl) row.

Left Front
Next row (WS) K32 (34, 37), leave rem sts on hold for the back and right front. Work even in reverse St st until armhole measures 3 (3½, 4)"/7.5 (9, 10)cm, end with a RS (or purl) row.

NECK SHAPING
Next row (WS) Bind off 4 (4, 6) sts, k to end. Cont to shape neck by binding off 2 sts from neck edge once, then dec 1 st every other row 4 times—22 (24, 25) sts. Work even until armhole measures 5½ (6, 6½)"/14 (15, 16.5)cm. Place sts on holder.

Back
With WS facing, rejoin yarn and work the next 62 (68, 72) sts for back, leaving rem sts on hold for right front. Cont in reverse St st until armhole measures 5½ (6, 6½)"/12.5 (15, 16.5)cm. Place sts on holder.

Right Front
With WS facing, rejoin yarn to rem sts for right front and cont in reverse St st until armhole measures 3 (3½, 4)"/7.5

Gauge
20 sts and 26 rows to 4"/10cm over reverse St st, after blocking, using larger needles.
Take time to check gauge.

(9, 10)cm, end with a WS (or knit) row.

NECK SHAPING
Next row (RS) Bind off 4 (4, 6) sts, p to end. Complete as for left front neck shaping.

JOIN SHOULDERS
Beg at armhole edge, join back and front pieces at left shoulder using 3-needle bind-off, bind off center 18 (20, 22) back sts for back neck, join back and front pieces at right shoulder using 3-needle bind-off.

Sleeves
With smaller needles, cast on 32 (34, 37) sts. Knit 5 rows.
Change to larger needles. Beg with a WS (or knit) row, work in reverse St st, inc 1 st each side every 4th row 12 (13, 14) times—56 (60, 65) sts.
Work even until piece measures 8½

(10½, 11½)"/21.5 (26.5, 29)cm from beg. Bind off.

Finishing
Block pieces to measurements.
Sew sleeves to armhole openings.
Sew sleeve seams.

NECKBAND
With smaller needle and RS facing, pick up and k 15 (15, 17) sts from the right front neck edge, 18 (20, 22) sts from the back neck, 15 (15, 17) sts from the left front neck edge—48 (50, 56) sts.
Knit 1 row, inc 4 sts across the back neck sts—52 (54, 60) sts.
Knit 4 rows more. Bind off.

LEFT FRONT EDGE
With smaller needles, from the RS, pick up and k 53 (57, 60) sts. Knit 5 rows. Bind off.

RIGHT FRONT EDGE
With smaller needles from the RS, pick up and k 53 (57, 60) sts. Knit 1 row.
Buttonhole row (RS) K5 (4, 2), [yo, k2tog, k7 (8, 9)] 5 times, yo, k2tog, k1. Knit 3 rows more. Bind off.
Sew buttons opposite buttonholes. ∎

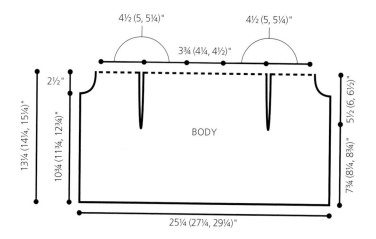
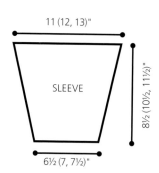

Bubble Blanket

Wrap little ones up in bold blocks of color and texture.
This blanket is worked in a slip-stitch pattern, using just one color per row.

DESIGNED BY KATHARINE HUNT

Knitted Measurements
28 x 35"/71 x 89cm

Materials
■ 4 3½oz/100g skeins (each approx 213yd/195m) of Cascade Yarns *Pacific* (acrylic/superwash merino wool) in #02 White (A) **(4)**
■ 1 skein each #52 Geranium (B) and #26 Lavender (C)
■ One pair size 6 (4mm) needles, *or size to obtain gauge*
■ One size E/4 (3.5mm) crochet hook
■ Removable stitch marker

Notes
1) Carry contrast color not in use along side of work.
2) Slip all sts purlwise.
3) Carry yarn loosely behind sl sts to keep to gauge.
4) This pat st tends to pucker, but will smooth out when blocking to measurements.

Pattern Stitch
(over a multiple of 8 sts plus 5)
Row 1 (RS) With B or C, k1, *sl 3 wyib, k5; rep from * to last 4 sts, sl 3 wyib, k1.
Row 2 (WS) P1, *sl 3 wyif, p5; rep from * to last 4 sts, sl 3 wyif, p1.
Rows 3–6 Rep rows 1 and 2 twice more.
Rows 7–10 With A, knit.
Row 11 With B or C, *k5, sl 3 wyib; rep from *, end k5.
Row 12 *P5, sl 3 wyif; rep from *, end p5.
Rows 13–16 Rep rows 11 and 12 twice more.
Rows 17–20 With A, knit.
Rep rows 1–20 for pat st.

Blanket
With A, cast on 147 sts. Work in garter st (k every row) as foll:
Row 1 (RS) K2, ssk, k to last 3 sts, k2tog, k2.
Row 2 Knit.
Rows 3–14 Rep rows 1 and 2 six times more —133 sts.
Knit 2 rows even.

BEGIN PATTERN STITCH
**With B, work rows 1–20 of pat st twice, then rows 1–6 once more. Cut B.
With A, knit 8 rows.
With C, work rows 1–20 of pat st twice, then rows 1–6 once more. Cut C.*
With A, knit 8 rows.**
Rep from ** to ** once more, then rep from ** to * once more.
With A, knit 2 rows.
Inc row (RS) K2, M1, k to last 2 sts, M1, k2.
Next row (WS) Knit.
Rep last 2 rows 6 times more —147 sts.
Bind off.

SIDE BORDERS
With RS facing, crochet hook, and A, work a row of sl st along one side edge of blanket (approx 170 sts). Turn. Working through back lp, work sl st in each sl st. Turn. Slip last lp to needle and pick up and k 1 st in back lp of each sl st. Knit 1 row on WS.
Inc row (RS) K2, M1, k to last 2 sts, M1, k2.
Next row (WS) Knit.
Rep last 2 rows 6 times more, end with a RS row—184 sts.
Bind off on WS.
Rep on opposite side.

Finishing
With A, sew 4 mitered corners tog. Weave in ends. Block to measurements. ■

Gauge
22 sts and 40 rows to 4"/10cm over pat st using size 6 (4mm) needles.
Take time to check gauge.

Cat Hat

Pointy ears, button eyes, and an embroidered face add character to this simple seed-stitch hat.

DESIGNED BY VALENTINA DEVINE

Sizes
Instructions are written for sizes Toddler (Child). Shown in size Child.

Knitted Measurements
Brim circumference 15½ (17½)"/39.5 (44.5)cm
Length 5½ (6½)"/14 (16.5)cm

Materials
▪ 1 3½oz/100g skein (each approx 213yd/195m) of Cascade Yarns *Pacific* (acrylic/superwash merino wool) in #61 Silver (A) (4)
▪ Small amount in #48 Black (B)
▪ One pair size 7 (4.5mm) needles, *or size to obtain gauge*
▪ Two ½"/13mm buttons
▪ Embroidery needle

Hat
With A, cast on 66 (74) sts.
Row 1 (RS) *K1, p1; rep from * to end.
Row 2 P the knit sts and k the purl sts.
Rep row 2 for seed stitch until piece measures 5½ (6½)"/14 (16.5)cm from beg. Bind off loosely in pat.

Finishing
Fold hat in half widthwise and sew bound-off edges together for top of hat.

Sew side seam.
Using photo as guide, embroider a diagonal line with B for each ear, beg at side edge approx 1½"/4cm from top corner, and working to upper edge approx 2"/5cm from corner.
With B, embroider a nose at center with lower edge approx 1¼"/3cm from cast-on edge, working a series of satin sts from 3 points of a triangle to form nose shape. With B, embroider whiskers on each side of nose using straight stitches.
Sew buttons for eyes approx 1½"/4cm above nose. ▪

Gauge
17 sts and 28 rows to 4"/10cm over seed stitch using size 7 (4.5mm) needles. *Take time to check gauge.*

Eyelet Cardi

This cardigan is a little ray of sunshine! It's perfect for layering over spring dresses or for a bit of brightness year round.

DESIGNED BY LISA CRAIG

Sizes
Instructions are written for sizes 2 (4, 6). Shown in size 4.

Knitted Measurements
Chest (closed) 26 (28, 30)"/66 (71, 76)cm
Length 13½ (14½, 15¾)"/34 (37, 40)cm
Upper arm 9¼ (11, 12)"/23 (28, 30.5)cm

Materials
- 3 (3, 4) 3½ oz/100 g skeins (each approx 213yd/195m) of Cascade Yarns *Pacific* (acrylic/superwash merino wool) in #13 Gold ④
- One pair each sizes 7 and 8 (4.5 and 5mm) needles, *or size to obtain gauge*
- Stitch holders
- Stitch markers
- Five ¹¹/₁₆"/18mm buttons

K1, P1 Rib
(over an odd number of sts).
Row 1 (RS) *K1, p1; rep from *, end k1.
Row 2 *P1, k1; rep from *, end p1.
Rep these 2 rows for k1, p1 rib.

Eyelet Pattern
(over an even number of sts)
Row 1 (RS) Knit.
Row 2 (WS) Purl.

Rows 3, 5, and 7 Knit.
Rows 4 and 6 Purl.
Row 8 (WS) Knit.
Row 9 K1, *yo, k2tog; rep from *, end k1.
Row 10 (WS) Knit.
Rep rows 1–10 for eyelet pat.

Back
With smaller needles, cast on 61 (65, 71) sts. Work in k1, p1 rib for 1¼"/3cm, inc 1 st at center of the last WS row—62 (66, 72) sts.

Change to larger needles.
Work in eyelet pat until piece measures 13 (14, 15¼)"/33 (35.5, 39)cm from beg, end with a pat row 6 or 8.

SHOULDER SHAPING
Bind off 8 (9, 10) sts at beg of next 2 rows, then 8 (8, 10) sts at beg of next 2 rows. Sl the rem 30 (32, 32) sts to holder for back neck.

Left Front
With smaller needles, cast on 34 (36, 40) sts.
Row 1 (RS) K1, [p1, k1] 14 (15, 17) times, k5 (center front band).
Row 2 (WS) K5, p1, [k1, p1] 14 (15, 17) times.
Rep these 2 rows for 1¼"/3cm, inc 1 st at end of the last WS row—35 (37, 41) sts.
Change to larger needles.
Next row (RS) Work in eyelet pat over first 30 (32, 36) sts, work in garter st (k every row) over last 5 sts for center front band.
Cont in pat as established until piece measures 11 (12, 13¼)"/28 (30.5, 33.5)cm from beg, end with a WS row.

NECK SHAPING
Next row (RS) Work in pat to last 7 sts, k2tog (neck dec), sl rem 5 sts to a st

Gauge
19 sts and 30 rows to 4"/10cm over eyelet pat using larger needles.
Take time to check gauge.

Eyelet Cardigan

holder, turn.

**Cont in eyelet pat, dec 1 st at neck edge (beg of WS rows or end of RS rows) *every* row 13 (14, 15) times—16 (17, 20) sts. Work even until piece measures 13 (14, 15¼)"/33 (35.5, 39)cm from beg.

SHOULDER SHAPING

Bind off 8 (9, 10) sts at beg of next RS row, then bind off rem 8 (8, 10) sts at beg of next RS row.

Place markers for 4 buttons on the front band, the first one at ½"/1.5cm from the lower edge, the last one at 2 (2¼, 2½)"/5 (5.5, 6.5)cm from top edge, and the other 2 spaced evenly between.

Right Front

With smaller needles, cast on 34 (36, 40) sts.
Row 1 (RS) K5, k1, [p1, k1] 14 (15, 17) times.
Row 2 P1, [k1, p1] 14 (15, 17) times, k5.
Rep row 1 once more.
Buttonhole row (RS) K1, k2tog, yo (for buttonhole), k2, work in rib to end.
Rep rows 1 and 2 until there are same number of rows as left front rib band, inc 1 st at beg of the last WS row—35 (37, 41) sts.
Change to larger needles.
Cont in garter st on first 5 sts and eyelet band pat on rem 30 (32, 36) sts, AT THE SAME TIME, work the buttonhole row opposite markers, until piece measures 11 (12, 13¼)"/28 (30.5, 33.5)cm from beg, end with a WS row.

NECK SHAPING

Next row (RS) K5 and sl these sts to a st holder, k2tog (neck dec), work to end.
Beg at **, complete neck shaping as for left front, working neck dec at beg of RS rows or end of WS rows.

SHOULDER SHAPING

Bind off 8 (9, 10) sts at beg of next WS row, then bind off rem 8 (8, 10) sts at beg of next WS row.

Sleeves

With smaller needles, cast on 29 (35, 39) sts. Work in k1, p1 rib for 1¼"/3cm, inc 3 sts evenly spaced across last WS row—32 (38, 42) sts.
Change to larger needles.
Work in eyelet pat for 4 rows.
Inc 1 st each side of next row, then rep inc every 6th row 5 (6, 6) times more—44 (52, 56) sts.
Work even until piece measures 7½ (9½, 10½)"/19 (24, 26.5) cm from beg.
Bind off.

Finishing

Weave in ends and block pieces to measurements. Sew shoulder seams. Pm at 4¼ (5½, 6)"/11.5 (14, 15)cm down from shoulder seams on front and back.
Sew bound-off edge of sleeves to armholes between markers.
Sew side and sleeve seams.

NECKBAND

With RS facing and smaller needles, k5 from right front holder, pick up and k 24 sts from shaped front neck edge, k sts from back neck holder, dec 1 st at center for 29 (31, 31) sts, k24 from shaped front neck edge, k5 from left front holder—87 (89, 89) sts.
Row 1 (WS) K6, *p1, k1; rep from * to last 6 sts, end k6.
Row 2 (RS) K5, *p1, k1; rep from * to last 6 sts, end p1, k5.
Next row Rep row 1.
Buttonhole row K1, k2tog, yo, k2, work as for row 2 to end.

Work 4 more rows in pat as established. Bind off in pat.
Sew buttons opposite buttonholes. ■

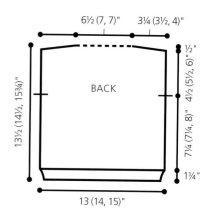

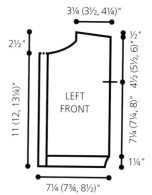

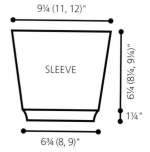

Cable Bear Poncho

Grownups will enjoy knitting the lush cables on this easy-to-wear poncho, while kids will love its snuggly hood and teddy-bear ears.

DESIGNED BY AUDREY DRYSDALE

Size
Instructions are written for size 4–6.

Knitted Measurements
Width 20"/51cm
Length 18"/45.5cm

Materials
- 5 3½oz/100g skeins (each approx 213yd/195m) of Cascade Yarns *Pacific* (acrylic/superwash merino wool) in #61 Silver (**4**)
- One pair each sizes 7 and 8 (4.5 and 5mm) needles, *or size to obtain gauge*
- Cable needle (cn)
- Removable stitch markers

3-Needle Bind-Off
1) Hold right sides of pieces together on two needles. Insert third needle knitwise into first st on each needle and wrap yarn knitwise.
2) Knit these two sts together and drop them from the needles. *Knit the next two sts together in the same manner.
3) Pass first st on third needle over second st and off needle. Rep from * in step 2 across row until all sts are bound off.

Stitch Glossary
RT (right twist) K 2nd st on LH needle, do *not* drop from needle, k first st on LH needle, and let both drop from needle.
2-st RC Sl 1 st to cn, hold to *back*; k1, k1 from cn.
2-st LC Sl 1 st to cn, hold to *front*; k1, k1 from cn.
3-st RPC Sl 1 st to cn, hold to *back*; k2, p1 from cn.

3-st LPC Sl 2 sts to cn, hold to *front*; p1, k2 from cn.
4-st RC Sl 2 sts to cn, hold to *back*; k2, k2 from cn.
4-st LC Sl 2 sts to cn, hold to *front*; k2, k2 from cn.

Double Seed Stitch
(over a multiple of 4 sts plus 2)
Row 1 (RS) K2, *p2, k2; rep from * to end.
Row 2 P2, *k2, p2; rep from * to end.
Row 3 Rep row 2.
Row 4 Rep row 1.
Rep rows 1–4 for double seed st.

Moss Stitch
(over a multiple of 2 sts plus 1)
Row 1 (RS) K1, *p1, k1; rep from * to end.
Row 2 P1, *k1, p1; rep from * to end.
Row 3 Rep row 2.
Row 4 Rep row 1.
Rep rows 1–4 for moss st.

Back
With smaller needles, cast on 111 sts.
Row 1 (RS) K1, *p1, k1; rep from * to end.
Row 2 P1, *k1, p1; rep from * to end.
Rep last 2 rows for k1, p1 rib for 2½"/6.5cm, end with a RS row.
Inc row (WS) Work 17 sts in rib, [M1,

Gauge
19 sts and 27 rows to 4"/10cm over double seed st using larger needles.
Take time to check gauge.

Cable Bear Poncho

work 13 sts in rib] 7 times, k3—118 sts. Change to larger needles.

BEGIN PATTERNS
Row 1 (RS) Work in moss st over 7 sts, *work Cable Panel A over 14 sts, work in double seed st over 14 sts, work Cable Panel A over 14 sts*, work Cable Panel B over 20 sts, rep from * to * once more, work in moss st over 7 sts.
Cont in pats as established until rows 1–26 of Cable Panel B have been worked 3 times, then work rows 1–16 once more. Piece measures approx 16½"/42cm from beg.

SHOULDER SHAPING
Bind off 8 sts at beg of next 8 rows, then 7 sts at beg of next 2 rows.
Bind off rem 40 sts.

Front
Work as for back until rows 1–26 of Cable Panel B have been worked 3 times, then work rows 1 and 2 once more. Piece measures approx 14½"/37cm from beg.

NECK SHAPING
Next row (RS) Work in pat over 47 sts, join 2nd ball of yarn and bind off center 24 sts, work in pat to end of row.
Working both sides at once, dec 1 st at each neck edge *every* row 3 times, then every other row 5 times, AT THE SAME TIME, when piece measures same as back to shoulder, shape shoulders as for back.

Hood
With smaller needles, cast on 121 sts. Work 6 rows in k1, p1 rib, inc 1 st at center of last row—122 sts.
Change to larger needles. Work 4 rows in double seed stitch.

Cont in pat, dec 1 st each side of next row, then every other row 5 times, then every 4th row 6 times—98 sts.
Work even in pat until piece measures 9½"/24cm from beg, end with a WS row. Divide sts evenly on 2 needles. Fold hood in half and join back seam using 3-needle bind-off.

Ears
With larger needles, cast on 14 sts. Work 8 rows in double seed stitch. Dec 1 st each side of next row, then every other row twice more—8 sts. Work 1 row even. Place marker on last st of row to mark halfway point. Inc 1 st each side of next row, then every

other row twice more—14 sts.
Work 7 rows even in pat. Bind off in pat. Fold ear along marked row. Sew sides and bottom edge. Remove marker. Repeat for second ear.

Finishing
Weave in ends and block pieces to measurements. Sew shoulder seams. Sew hood to neck edge so that hood fronts meet at center front neck, easing in if necessary. Sew one ear to each side of hood, using photo as guide.
Place markers at front and back side edges approx 7½"/19cm from each shoulder. Sew side seams from lower edge to markers. ■

CABLE PANEL A

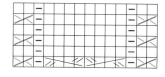

14 sts

CHART KEY

☐ k on RS, p on WS

– p on RS, k on WS

⧓ RT

⧄ 2-st RC

⧅ 2-st LC

3-st RPC

3-st LPC

4-st RC

4-st LC

CABLE PANEL B

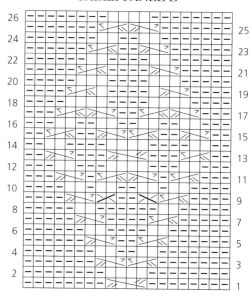

20 sts

23 Textured Cowls

Worked seamlessly in the round, these chunky reversible cowls
knit up so quickly, you can make one in every color!

DESIGNED BY LORI STEINBERG

Knitted Measurements
Circumference 20"/51cm
Length 6"/15cm

Materials
■ 1 3½oz/100g skein (each approx
120yd/110m) of Cascade Yarns *Pacific
Chunky* (acrylic/superwash merino wool)
in #84 Persimmon or #95 Lime Green
or #106 Carmine Rose ⑤
■ One set (5) size 10½ (6.5mm)
double-pointed needles (dpn),
or size to obtain gauge
■ Stitch marker

Texture Pattern
(over a multiple of 6 sts)
Rnd 1 *K3, p3; rep from * around.
Rnd 2 *P1, k1; rep from * around.
Rep rnds 1 and 2 for texture pat.

Cowl
Cast on 60 sts. Divide sts evenly over 4
needles (15 sts per needle). Join, being
careful not to twist sts, and pm for beg
of rnd. Work in texture pattern until cowl
measures 6"/15cm from beg, end with
rnd 2. Bind off in pat.

Finishing
Weave in ends and block lightly to
measurements. ■

Gauge
12 sts and 18 rnds to 4"/10cm over texture pat using size 10½ (6.5mm) needles.
Take time to check gauge.

Heart Hat

A string of colorwork hearts encircles this sweet hat trimmed with a trio of fluffy pompoms.

DESIGNED BY DIANE ZANGL

Knitted Measurements
Brim circumference 17"/43cm
Length 7½"/19cm

Materials
■ 1 3½oz/100g skein (each approx 213yd/195m) of Cascade Yarns *Pacific* (acrylic/superwash merino wool) each in #51 Honeysuckle Pink (A) and #01 Cream (B) (4)
■ Size 6 (4mm) circular needle, 16"/40cm long, *or size to obtain gauge*
■ One set (4) size 6 (4mm) double-pointed needles (dpn)
■ Stitch marker

Notes
1) Yarn is held double throughout.
2) Chart is worked in St st (k every rnd). When changing colors, twist yarns on WS to prevent holes in work. Carry color not in use *loosely* across back of work to avoid puckering.

Hat
With A held double and circular needle, cast on 72 sts. Join, taking care not to twist sts, and pm for beg of rnd.
Rnd 1 *K1, p1; rep from * around.

Rep rnd 1 for k1, p1 rib for 4 rnds more.
Inc rnd [K9, M1] 8 times—80 sts.
Knit 2 rnds.

BEGIN CHART
Rnd 1 Adding B held double, work 10-st rep 8 times around. Cont to work chart in this way through rnd 15.
Work even in St st with A only until hat measures 7"/18cm from beg.

CROWN SHAPING
Note Change to dpn when sts no longer fit comfortably on circular needle.
Dec rnd *K2tog; rep from * around—40 sts.
Next rnd Knit.
Rep last 2 rnds once more—20 sts.
Rep dec rnd twice more—5 sts. Cut yarn and pull through rem sts, draw up and secure.

EARFLAPS
Locate beg of rnd at cast-on edge.
Place markers in 9th st each side of beg of rnd, then 11 sts beyond first markers on each side. With RS facing, dpn, and A, pick up and k 12 sts between markers on one side.
Next 11 rows Sl 1, k11.
Dec row Sl 1, k2tog, k to end—1 st dec'd.
Rep dec row *every* row 8 times more—3 sts.

*Next row (RS) Knit. Slide sts back to beg of needle to work next row from the RS. Bring yarn around from back. Rep from * until I-cord measures 6"/15cm.
Next row K3tog. Fasten off last st and secure end inside cord. Rep for 2nd earflap.

Finishing
With B, make three 1½"/4cm pompoms. Secure one to top of hat and one to the end of each I-cord tie. Weave in ends. ■

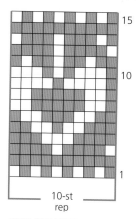

COLOR KEY
■ A
□ B

10-st rep

Gauge
19 sts and 22 rnds to 4"/10cm over St st using size 6 (4mm) needles and 2 strands of yarn held together.
Take time to check gauge.

Fair Isle Detail Mittens

They'll never lose a mitten again! Connected by a quick-to-crochet cord, it's easy to keep these colorwork-detail mittens on hand.

DESIGNED BY LORI STEINBERG

Sizes
Instructions are written for sizes 2 (4–6). Shown in size 2.

Knitted Measurements
Hand circumference 5½ (6½)"/14 (16.5)cm
Length 6 (7)"/15 (18)cm

Materials
■ 1 3½oz/100g skein (each approx 213yd/195m) of Cascade Yarns *Pacific* (acrylic/superwash merino wool) each in #61 Silver (A) and #93 Methyl Blue (B) 〖4〗
■ One set (4) size 7 (4.5mm) double-pointed needles (dpn), *or size to obtain gauge*
■ Size H/8 (5mm) crochet hook
■ Stitch markers
■ Scrap yarn

Mittens
With A, cast on 30 (36) sts. Divide sts evenly over 3 needles—10 (12) sts per needle. Join, taking care not to twist sts, and pm for beg of rnd.
Rnd 1 *K1, p2; rep from * around.
Rep rnd 1 for k1, p2 rib for 2"/5cm.
Knit 1 (2) rnd(s).
Inc rnd [Kfb] twice, k to end—32 (38) sts.
Knit 3 rnds.
Inc rnd Kfb, k2, kfb, k to end—34 (40) sts.

Next rnd Place first 6 sts on scrap yarn for thumb, cast on 1 st, place new marker for beg of rnd, cast on 1 st, k to end—30 (36) sts.

BEGIN FAIR ISLE PATTERN
Rnd 1 *K1 A, k1 B; rep from * around.
Rnd 2 *K1 B, k1 A; rep from * around.
Rep rnds 1 and 2 twice more, then rep rnd 1 once more. Cut A.
With B only, knit 3 (5) rnds.

SHAPE TOP
For size 4–6 only
Dec rnd [K4, k2tog] 6 times—30 sts.
Knit 2 rnds.

For both sizes
Dec rnd [K4, k2tog] 5 times—25 sts.
Knit 2 rnds.
Dec rnd [K3, k2tog] 5 times—20 sts.
Knit 1 rnd.
Dec rnd [K2, k2tog] 5 times—15 sts.
Dec rnd [K1, k2tog] 5 times—10 sts.
Dec rnd [K2tog] 5 times—5 sts.
Cut yarn and pull through rem sts, draw up and secure.

THUMB
Place 6 thumb sts on dpn. With A, k6, pick up and k 4 sts along hand edge, pm for beg of rnd—10 sts.
Work in St st (k every rnd) until thumb measures 1¾ (2)"/4.5 (5)cm.
Dec rnd [K2tog] 5 times—5 sts.
Cut yarn and pull through rem sts, draw up and secure.

Finishing
With crochet hook and A, make a chain approx 36"/92cm long. Sl st in 1 loop of each ch. Fasten off.
Sew one end of cord to cast-on edge of each mitten, aligning with thumb.
Weave in ends. ■

Gauge
22 sts and 24 rnds to 4"/10cm over St st using size 7 (4.5mm) needles.
Take time to check gauge.

Fox Hat

With the warm earflaps on this clever hat, kids can stay toasty and outfox all the other kids on the playground.

DESIGNED BY AUDREY DRYSDALE

Knitted Measurements
Head circumference 17"/43cm
Length 7½"/19cm

Materials
- 1 3½oz/100g skein (each approx 120yd/110m) of Cascade Yarns *Pacific Chunky* (acrylic/superwash merino wool) each in #02 White (A), #43 Ruby (B), and #48 Black (C) **(5)**
- One pair size 10 (6mm) needles, *or size to obtain gauge*
- Tapestry needle
- Bobbins

Notes
1) Colorwork is done using the intarsia method. Use separate bobbins for each color section. Do *not* carry colors across WS of work.
2) Nose and eyes are worked in duplicate stitch after knitting is completed.
3) Mouth is embroidered after knitting is completed.

K1, P1 Rib
(over an odd number of sts)
Row 1 (RS) K2, *p1, k1; rep from * to end.
Row 2 K the knit sts and p the purl sts.
Rep row 2 for k1, p1 rib.

Hat
With A, cast on 63 sts. Work 4 rows in k1, p1 rib, end with a WS row. Beg with a knit (RS) row, work 6 rows in St st (k on RS, p on WS).

BEGIN CHART
Note Beg chart at row 5. Rows 1–4 of chart are worked in St st with A

only. Nose and eyes will be worked in duplicate st after hat is complete.
Next row (RS) K20 with A, pm, work row 5 of chart over 23 sts, pm, k20 with A. Cont to work chart over center 23 sts between markers as established and rem sts in St st with A, through chart row 18. Cut A.
Next row (RS) With B, knit.
Dec row (WS) With B, k1, *k2tog, k6; rep from * to last 6 sts, k2tog, k4—55 sts.

SHAPE CROWN
Cont with B only in garter st (k every row) to end of hat as foll:
Dec row 1 (RS) K1, *k2tog, k7; rep from * to end—49 sts.
Rows 2–4 Knit.
Dec row 5 (RS) K1, *k2tog, k6; rep from * to end—43 sts.
Row 6 and all WS rows Knit.
Dec row 7 K1, *k2tog, k5; rep from * to end—37 sts.
Dec row 9 K1, *k2tog, k4; rep from * to end—31 sts.
Dec row 11 K1, *k2tog, k3; rep from * to end—25 sts.
Dec row 13 K1, *k2tog, k2; rep from * to end—19 sts.

Gauge
15 sts and 20 rows to 4"/10cm over St st using size 10 (6mm) needles. *Take time to check gauge.*

Fox Hat

Dec row 15 K1, *k2tog; rep from * to end—10 sts.
Cut yarn, leaving a long tail. Thread tail through rem 10 sts and pull tightly to close.

Finishing

Sew center back seam.

FACE EMBROIDERY
With tapestry needle and C, foll chart for duplicate st embroidery of eyes and nose. Separate a small length of C into 2 plys. Using outline st, embroider mouth, using photo as guide.

OUTER EARS
With A, cast on 8 sts. Work 8 rows in garter st.
Dec row (RS) K2tog, k to last 2 sts, ssk—6 sts.
Next row Knit.
Rep last 2 rows twice more—2 sts.
Next row K2tog. Fasten off.

INNER EARS
With A, cast on 6 sts. Work 6 rows in garter st.
Dec row (RS) K2tog, k to last 2 sts, ssk—4 sts.
Next row Knit.
Rep last 2 rows once more—2 sts.
Next row K2tog. Fasten off.
Sew inner ear to outer ear. Sew ears to hat, using photo as guide.

EAR FLAPS
With B, cast on 11 sts. Work 10 rows in garter st.
Dec row (RS) K2tog, k to last 2 sts, ssk—9 sts.
Next row Knit.
Rep last 2 rows 3 times more—3 sts.
Next row K3tog. Fasten off.

TIES
With B, cast on 35 sts. Bind off all sts knitwise.
Sew each tie to bottom of ear flap.
Sew ear flaps in position along last row of ribbing on WS of hat. ■

COLOR & STITCH KEY

☐ MC

■ k on RS with A

– k on WS with A

V duplicate stitch with B

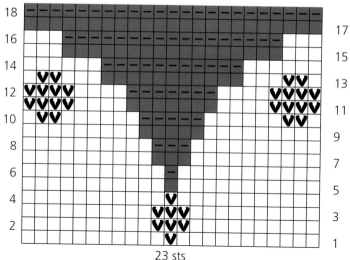

23 sts

Striped Cardigan

Six colors create graded stripes on this reverse-stockinette cardigan, with dotted lines in between.

DESIGNED BY YOKO HATTA

Sizes
Instructions are written for sizes 2 (4, 6). Shown in size 6.

Knitted Measurements
Chest (closed) 26½ (28½, 30¾)"/67 (72.5, 78)cm
Length 13½ (14½, 15½)"/34 (37, 39.5)cm
Upper arm 10½ (11½, 12½)"/26.5 (29, 32)cm

Materials
▪ 1 3½oz/100g skein (each approx 213yd/195m) of Cascade Yarns *Pacific* (acrylic/superwash merino wool) each in #20 Light Blue (A), #97 Dark Green (B), #63 Olive (C), #12 Yellow (D), #65 Medium Blue (E), and #64 Blue (F) 〔4〕
▪ One pair each sizes 4 and 6 (3.5 and 4mm) needles, *or size to obtain gauge*
▪ One extra size 6 (4mm) needle for 3-needle bind off
▪ Stitch holders
▪ Six ⅝"/15mm buttons

3-Needle Bind-Off
1) Hold right sides of pieces together on two needles. Insert third needle knitwise into first st of each needle, and wrap yarn knitwise.
2) Knit these two sts together and drop them off the needles. *Knit the next two

sts together in the same manner.
3) Slip first st on 3rd needle over 2nd st and off needle. Rep from * in step 2 across row until all sts are bound off.

Stripe Pattern
Row 1 (WS) With B, knit.
Row 2 (RS) With B, purl.
Row 3 With C, knit.
Row 4 With C, purl.
Row 5 With D, knit.
Row 6 With D, purl.
Row 7 With E, knit.
Row 8 With E, purl.
Row 9 With F, knit.
Row 10 With F, purl.
Row 11 With A, knit.
Row 12 With A, purl.
Rep rows 1–12 for stripe pat.

Body
With smaller needles and A, cast on 124 (134, 144) sts. Knit 5 rows.
Change to larger needles.

BEGIN STRIPE PATTERN
Beg with WS row 1 of stripe pat, rep rows 1–12 of stripe pat until piece measures 8½ (9, 9½)"/21.5 (23, 24)cm from beg, end with a RS stripe row.

LEFT FRONT
Next row (WS) K31 (34, 36), leave rem sts on hold for the back and right front. Work even in stripe pat on these sts for 2½ (3, 3½)"/6.5 (7.5, 9)cm from the armhole, end with a RS (or purl) row.

NECK SHAPING
Cont in stripe pat, work as foll:
Next row (WS) Bind off 4 (4, 5) sts, k to end.
Cont to shape neck, binding off 2 sts from neck edge once, then dec 1 st every

Gauge
19 sts and 26 rows to 4"/10cm over St st (after blocking) using larger needles.
Take time to check gauge.

other row 4 times—21 (24 25) sts.
Work even until armhole measures
5 (5½, 6)"/12.5 (14, 15)cm. Place sts on
holder for shoulder.

BACK
Rejoin yarn from the WS and work 62
(66, 72) sts for back, cont in stripe pat
until armhole measures 5 (5½, 6)"/12.5
(14, 15)cm. Place sts on holder.

RIGHT FRONT
Rejoin yarn from the WS to sts for right
front and cont in stripe pat until armhole
measures 2½ (3, 3½)"/6.5 (7.5, 9)cm, end
with a WS (or knit) row.

NECK SHAPING
Next row (RS) Bind off 4 (4, 5) sts, p to
end.
Complete as for left front neck shaping.
Slip the 21 (24, 25) sts from right back to
larger needle, join these sts tog with the
right front shoulder sts using the 3-nee-
dle bind-off method. Join the 21 (24, 25)
sts from left shoulder in same way.

Sleeves
With smaller needles and A, cast on 34
(37, 38) sts.
Knit 5 rows. Change to larger needles.

BEGIN STRIPE PATTERN
Beg with row 1 of pattern, rep rows 1–12
of stripe pat, inc 1 st each side of next
row then every 6th row 8 (9, 11) times
more—52 (57, 62) sts.
Work even until piece measures 8½
(10½, 11½)"/21.5 (26.5, 29)cm from beg.
Bind off.
Sew sleeves to armhole openings.
Sew sleeve seams.

Finishing
Weave in ends and block sweater to
measurements.

NECKBAND
With RS facing, smaller needles, and A,
pick up and k 16 (16, 17) sts from the right
front neck edge, k18 (20, 22) from the
back neck holder, pick up and k 16 (16,
17) sts from the left front neck edge—50
(52, 56) sts. Knit 5 rows. Bind off.

RIGHT FRONT EDGE
With smaller needles and A, from the RS,
pick up and k 50 (54, 59) sts.
Knit 7 rows. Bind off.

LEFT FRONT EDGE
With smaller needles and A, from the RS,
pick up and k 50 (54, 59) sts. Knit 1 row.
Buttonhole row (RS) K2, [yo, k2tog, k6
(7, 8)] 5 times, yo, k2tog, k6 (5, 5).
Knit 5 rows, then bind off all sts.

Sew buttons opposite buttonholes. ∎

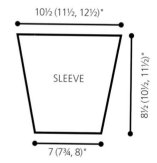

10½ (11½, 12½)"

SLEEVE

8½ (10½, 11½)"

7 (7¾, 8)"

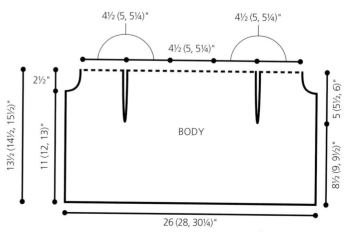

4½ (5, 5¼)"   4½ (5, 5¼)"

4½ (5, 5¼)"

2½"

13½ (14½, 15½)"

11 (12, 13)"

BODY

5 (5½, 6)"

8½ (9, 9½)"

26 (28, 30¼)"

Bow Headband

Put a bow on it! This simple seed-stitch headband is dressed up with a jaunty off-center bow.

DESIGNED BY BECKY KEVELSON

Sizes
Instructions are written for sizes 2 (4, 6). Shown in size 2.

Knitted Measurements
Head circumference 14 (16, 18)"/35.5 (40.5, 45.5)cm

Materials
- 1 3½oz/100g skein (each approx 213yd/195m) of Cascade Yarns *Pacific* (acrylic/superwash merino wool) in #18 Cotton Candy (4)
- One pair size 7 (4.5mm) needles, *or size to obtain gauges*
- Elastic thread (optional)

Note
If desired, work a strand of elastic thread along with the main yarn when working the band for a more stretchy fabric.

Band
Cast on 13 sts.
Row 1 *K1, p1; rep from *, end k1.
Rep row 1 for seed stitch until piece measures 14 (16, 18)"/35.5 (40.5, 45.5)cm, or desired head circumference.
Bind off in pat.

Bow
Cast on 2 sts.
Row 1 (RS) K1, kfb —3 sts.
Row 2 Purl.
Row 3 K to last st, kfb —1 st inc'd.
Row 4 Purl.
Rep last 2 rows until there are 18 sts on needle.
Cont in St st until piece measures

16"/40.5cm from beg, end with a WS row.
Next row (RS) K2tog, k to end—1 st dec'd.
Next row Purl.
Rep last 2 rows until there are 2 sts on needle. Bind off.

Finishing
Weave in ends and block pieces lightly. Fold band in half and sew cast-on and bound-off edges together for back seam.

SHAPE BOW
Lay bow piece flat. Place markers 4"/10cm in from each edge. Fold bow piece in half with RS facing. Pinch markers tog and bring center fold to markers. Make sure points of edges point down and out from center of bow. Pin bow in place to keep shape, then sew bow to secure.
Wrap a single strand of yarn 8 times around center of the bow (see picture).

PLACE BOW
Measure 6½ (7½, 8½)"/16.5 (19, 21.5)cm from the seam on the band and sew bow in place. Tack down loops and tails of bow in place, as desired (see picture). ■

Gauges
20 sts and 24 rows to 4"/10cm over St st using size 7 (4.5mm) needles.
20 sts and 32 rows to 4"/10cm over seed stitch using size 7 (4.5mm) needles. *Take time to check gauges.*

29

Turtleneck Poncho

Worked in a beautiful textured stitch pattern,
this poncho looks adorable and will fit growing kids for years to come.

DESIGNED BY IRINA POLUDNENKO

Sizes
Instructions are written for sizes 2 (4, 6).
Shown in size 4.

Knitted Measurements
Chest 31 (34, 36)"/79 (86.5, 91.5)cm
Length 12½ (13½, 14½)"/32 (34.5, 37)cm

Materials
■ 2 3½oz/100g skeins (each approx
213yd/195m) of Cascade Yarns *Pacific*
(acrylic/superwash merino wool)
in #15 Taupe (A) (**4**)
■ 1 skein in #98 Deep Sea Coral (B)
■ One pair size 8 (5mm) needles,
or size to obtain gauge
■ Size 8 (5mm) circular needle,
16"/40cm long
■ Removable stitch markers

Note
Poncho is knit from back hem to front
hem in one piece.

Garter Rib
(over a multiple of 4 sts plus 2)
Row 1 (RS) K2, *p2, k2; rep from * to end.
Row 2 Purl.
Rep rows 1 and 2 for garter rib.

Textured Stitch Pattern
(over a multiple of 4 sts plus 2)
Row 1 (RS) K1, *k2, k2tog and leave sts
on needle, k first st again, drop both sts tog
from LH needle; rep from * to last st, k1.
Row 2 Purl.
Row 3 K1, *k2tog and leave sts on
needle, k first st again, drop both sts tog
from LH needle, k2; rep from * to last st, k1.

Row 4 Purl.
Rep rows 1–4 for textured st pat.

Poncho
With A, cast on 82 (90, 94) sts. Work in
garter rib for 1½"/4cm, end with a WS row.
Beg with row 1, work in textured st pat
until piece measures 12½ (13½, 14½)"/32
(34.5, 37)cm from beg, end with a WS
row, placing markers in first and last sts on
last row worked to mark shoulders.

DIVIDE FOR NECK OPENING
Next row (RS) Work 28 (30, 32) sts, join
a 2nd ball of yarn and bind off center 26
(30, 30) sts for back neck, work to end.
Working both sides at once, work 5 rows
even in pat, end with a WS row.

FRONT NECK SHAPING
Cont in pat, inc 1 st at each neck edge
every row 8 (10, 10) times, end with a
WS row—36 (40, 42) sts each side.

JOIN FRONTS
Next row (RS) Work first 36 (40, 42) sts,
cast on 10 sts for front neck, work rem
36 (40, 42) sts—82 (90, 94) sts.
Work even in pat until piece measures 11

Gauge
21 sts and 25 rows to 4"/10cm over textured st pat using size 8 (5mm) needles.
Take time to check gauge.

Turtleneck Poncho

(12, 13)"/28 (30.5, 33)cm from shoulder marker, end with a RS row.
Beg with row 2 (WS), work in garter rib for 1½"/4cm, end with a RS row. Bind off all sts loosely in rib.

Pockets

With B, cast on 22 sts. Work 6 rows in garter rib, end with a WS row.
Beg with row 1, work 10 rows in textured st pat, end with a WS row.
Dec 1 st at each end of next RS row, then every other row 9 times more, end with a RS row—12 sts.
Bind off all sts purlwise.

Finishing

Block to measurements.

ARMHOLE BANDS
Place markers on each side for armholes, 5 (5½, 6)"/12.5 (14, 15)cm down from shoulder markers.
Remove shoulder markers.
With RS facing and A, pick up and k 50 (54, 58) sts between armhole markers.
Beg with row 2 (WS), work 5 rows in

garter rib, end with a WS rows.
Bind off all sts in rib.
Sew side and armhole band seams.

TURTLENECK
With RS facing, circular needle, and B, starting at back neck, pick up and k 68 (76, 80) sts evenly around neck opening. Join and pm for beg of rnd.
Rnd 1 *K2, p2; rep from * around.
Rnd 2 Knit.
Rep rnds 1 and 2 until turtleneck measures 2"/5cm from pick up rnd, end with rnd 2.
Next rnd Purl.
Next rnd *P2, k2; rep from * around.
Rep last 2 rnds until turtleneck measures 6"/15cm from pick-up rnd. Bind off all sts loosely in rib.
Using photo as a guide, pin pockets to front with side edge of pocket approx 2"/5cm up from lower edge and cast-on edge of pocket approx 3 (3½, 4)"/7.5 (9, 10) cm from side seam.
Whipstitch side and bound-off edges of pocket to front, leaving cast-on edge open. ■

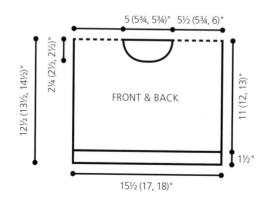

FRONT & BACK

5 (5¾, 5¾)"   5½ (5¾, 6)"

2¼ (2½, 2½)"

12½ (13½, 14½)"

11 (12, 13)"

1½"

15½ (17, 18)"

Eyelet Dress

Special occasion? Any child will feel fancy in this sweet dress with a ribbed yoke and buttons down the back.

DESIGNED BY YOKO HATTA

Sizes
Instructions are written for sizes 2 (4, 6). Shown in size 4.

Knitted Measurements
Lower Edge 36½ (40, 44½)"/92.5 (101.5, 113)cm
Chest 20½ (23, 26)"/52 (58.5, 66)cm
Length 18 (20, 22)"/45.5 (51, 56)cm

Materials
▪ 3 3½oz/100g skeins (each approx 213yd/195m) of Cascade Yarns *Pacific* (acrylic/superwash merino wool) in #01 Cream ④
▪ One each sizes 6 and 7 (4 and 4.5mm) circular needle, 20"/50cm long, *or size to obtain gauges*
▪ Size F/5 (3.75mm) crochet hook for button loops
▪ Three ⅝"/15mm buttons
▪ Stitch holders

Eyelet Pattern
(over a multiple of 10 sts plus 13)
Row 1 (RS) K10, *k2tog, yo, k8; rep from * to last 11 sts, k11.
Rows 2–8 Work in St st (k on RS, p on WS).
Row 9 K6, *k2tog, yo, k8; rep from * to last 7 sts, k2tog, yo, k5.
Rows 10–16 Work in St st.
Rep rows 1–16 for eyelet pat.

Note
Circular needles are used to accommodate the large number of sts. Dress is worked in one piece, back and forth in rows, and seamed at the center back to beg of placket.

Dress
With smaller needle, cast on 183 (203, 223) sts. Work in garter st (k every row) for 6 rows.
Change to larger needle.
Beg with a RS (or knit) row, work in St st for 6 rows.

BEGIN EYELET PATTERN
Work in eyelet pat until 16 rows of pat have been worked 4 times, then work rows 1–4 once more—piece measures approx 11½"/29cm from beg.

Ribbed Yoke
For size 2 only
Dec row (RS) K2, [k1, k2tog, k2tog] 35 times, k1, k2tog, k3—112 sts.
For size 4 only
Dec row (RS) K1, [k1, k2tog, k2tog, k1, k2tog] 25 times, k2—128 sts.

Gauges
20 sts and 28 rows to 4"/10cm over eyelet pat using larger needle.
22 sts and 28 rows to 4"/10cm over k2, p2 rib (slightly stretched) using larger needle. *Take time to check gauges.*

Eyelet Dress

For size 6 only
Dec row (RS) K6, [k1, k2tog, k2tog, k1, k2tog] 26 times, k2tog, k7—144 sts.
For all sizes
Next row (WS) P3, *k2, p2; rep from * to last 3 sts, p3.
Next row K3, *p2, k2; rep from * to last 3 sts, k3.
Rep last 2 rows for k2, p2 rib until ribbed yoke measures 2 (2½, 3)"/5 (6.5, 7.5)cm, end with a RS row.

DIVIDE FOR FRONT AND BACKS
Next row (WS) P3, [k2, p2] 6 (7, 8) times, k1—28 (32, 36) sts for right back, place these sts on a st holder; k1, [p2, k2] 13 (15, 17) times, p2, k1—56 (64, 72) sts for front; place rem 28 (32, 36) sts on a 2nd st holder for left back. Work on 56 (64, 72) front sts only as foll:

ARMHOLE SHAPING
Dec row 1 (RS) K2, ssk, cont in rib as established to last 4 sts, k2tog, k2.
Dec row 2 (WS) P2, p2tog, cont in rib as established to last 4 sts, ssp, p2.
Rep last 2 rows 0 (1, 2) times more—52 (56, 60) sts.
Next row (RS) K3, cont in rib to last 3 sts, k3. Cont in rib until armhole measures 2½ (3, 3½)"/6.5 (7.5, 9)cm, end with a WS row.

NECK SHAPING
Next row (RS) Work 12 sts, join 2nd ball of yarn and bind off center 28 (32, 36) sts in rib, work to end. Work 12 sts each side with separate balls of yarn for 2½"/6.5cm. Bind off sts each side in rib for shoulders.

Right Back
Sl 28 (32, 36) sts from right back holder to larger needle to work next row from RS.

ARMHOLE SHAPING
Next row (RS) K2, ssk, cont in rib as established to end.
Next row (WS) Rib to last 4 sts, ssp, p2. Rep last 2 rows 0 (1, 2) times more—26 (28, 30) sts.
Next row K3, cont in rib to end. Cont in rib as established until armhole measures 3½ (4, 4½)"/9 (10, 11.5)cm, end with a RS row.

NECK SHAPING
Next row (WS) Bind off 10 (12, 14) sts, rib to end.
Next row (RS) Rib to last 4 sts, k2tog, k2.
Next row P2, p2tog, cont in rib to end. Rep last 2 rows once more.
Work even in rib on rem 12 sts until armhole measures same length as front. Bind off sts for shoulder.

Left Back
Sl 28 (32, 36) sts from left back holder to larger needle to work next row from WS.
Next row (WS) K1, [p2, k2] 6 (7, 8) times, p3.

ARMHOLE SHAPING
Next row (RS) Cont in rib as established to last 4 sts, k2tog, k2.
Next row (WS) P2, p2tog, cont in rib to end. Rep last 2 rows 0 (1, 2) times more—26 (28, 30) sts.
Next row Cont in rib to last 3 sts, k3. Cont in rib as established until armhole measures 3½ (4, 4½)"/9 (10, 11.5)cm, end with a WS row.

NECK SHAPING
Next row (RS) Bind off 10 (12, 14) sts, rib to end.
Next row (WS) Rib to last 4 sts, ssp, p2.
Next row K2, ssk, cont in rib to end. Rep last 2 rows once more.

Work even in rib on rem 12 sts until armhole measures same length as front. Bind off sts for shoulder.

Finishing
Block lightly to measurements; do *not* block rib. Sew center back seam from lower edge to 2 (2½, 3)"/5 (6.5, 7.5)cm above ribbed yoke (see red line on schematic), leaving rem yoke open. Sew buttons to left back placket edge, with the first one just below first neck bind-off, the last one approx 3 rows above center back seam, and the 3rd one spaced evenly between.
BUTTON LOOPS
With RS facing and crochet hook, join yarn with sl st to top of right back placket, ch 5, [skip 2 or 3 rows along placket edge, work approx 5 sl sts along placket edge (or necessary number to match button placement), ch 5] twice, work sl st to end of placket. Fasten off. Weave in ends. ∎

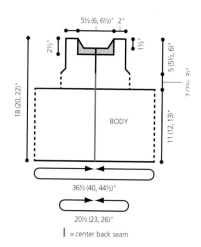

5½ (6, 6½)" 2"
2½"
1½"
5 (5½, 6)"
18 (20, 22)"
11 (12, 13)"
BODY
36½ (40, 44½)"
20½ (23, 26)"

| = center back seam

31 Doll Hair Hat

Kids will love getting all dolled up in this fun hat.
Knit one to match their favorite doll, or in any color of the rainbow!

DESIGNED BY BEA NARETTO

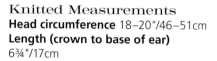

Knitted Measurements
Head circumference 18–20"/46–51cm
Length (crown to base of ear)
6¾"/17cm

Materials
- 2 3½oz/100g skeins (each approx 120yd/110m) of Cascade Yarns *Pacific Chunky* (acrylic/superwash merino wool) in #30 Latte ⑤
- One set (5) each sizes 8 and 11 (5 and 8mm) double-pointed needles (dpn), *or size to obtain gauge*
- Stitch markers
- Darning needle
- 23½"/60cm satin ribbon, ½"/1.5cm wide

Stitch Glossary
LS (loop stitch) K1, keeping st on LH needle, bring yarn forward, pass yarn over left thumb to make a loop, take yarn to the back, k same st again, sl st off LH needle, yo and pass the 2 sts just worked over this loop.
K1b Knit 1 in the row below.

Fisherman's Rib
Rnd 1 *K1, p1; rep from * around.
Rnd 2 *K1b, p1; rep from * around.
Rep rnds 1 and 2 for fisherman's rib.

Brim
With larger dpn, cast on 48 sts. Divide sts evenly over 3 needles. Join, taking care to not twist sts on needle, and pm for beg of rnd.
Rnd 1 *LS, p1; rep from * around.
Rep rnd 1 three times more.

Crown
With smaller dpn, work in fisherman's rib for 19 rnds.

CROWN SHAPING
Dec rnd 23 *SK2P, p1, [k1b, p1] 4 times; rep from * around—40 sts.
Rnd 24 *K1, p1; rep from * around.
Dec rnd 25 *SK2P, p1, [k1b, p1] 3 times; rep from * around—32 sts.
Rnd 26 *K1, p1; rep from * around.
Dec rnd 27 *SK2P, p1, [k1b, p1] twice; rep from * around—24 sts.
Rnd 28 *K1, p1; rep from * around.
Dec rnd 29 *SK2P, p1, k1b, p1; rep from * around—16 sts.
Rnd 30 *K1, p1; rep from * around.
Dec rnd 31 *SK2P, p1; rep from * around—8 sts.
Cut yarn, leaving a 12"/30cm tail. Thread tail though rem sts and cinch tightly to close.

Finishing
Weave in ends.

PONYTAIL (MAKE 2)
Cut 40 strands of yarn each approx 23½"/60cm long.
Hold all strands together, aligning ends. Place another piece of yarn around the middle of the strands and knot it, leaving long ends. Use long ends to secure ponytail to hat. Hold yarn together and wrap two other pieces of yarn around the ponytail, placing them approx 4"/10cm from the top and 3¼"/8cm from the bottom. With the satin ribbon, make 2 bows and secure to hat using photo as a guide. ∎

Gauge
16 sts and 26 rnds to 4"/10cm over fisherman's rib (unstretched) using smaller needles.
Take time to check gauge.

32 Bow Tie

This little bow tie is a cinch to knit and will turn any kid into a dapper gent.

DESIGNED BY MATTHEW SCHRANK

Sizes
Instructions are written for size 2 (4, 6). Shown in size 6.

Knitted Measurements
Neck circumference (buttoned) approx 10 (10½,11)"/25.5 (26.5, 28)cm
Bow width 4 (4½, 5)"/10 (11.5, 12.5)cm

Materials
- 1 3½oz/100g skein (each approx 213yd/195m) of Cascade Yarns *Pacific* (acrylic/superwash merino wool) in #56 Kelly Green
- One pair size 7 (4.5mm) needles, *or size to obtain gauge*
- One ½"/6mm button

Bow
Cast on 10 (12, 14) sts.
Row 1 *K1, p1; rep from * to end.
Row 2 *P1, k1; rep from * to end.
Rep rows 1 and 2 for seed st until piece measures 4 (4½, 5)"/10 (11.5, 12.5)cm from beg. Bind off in pat.

Button Band
Cast on 4 sts. Work in St st (k on RS, p on WS) for 10 (10½, 11)"/25.5 (26.5, 28cm, end with a WS row.
Buttonhole row (RS) K1, yo, k2tog, k1. Work even in St st for 1"/2.5cm more. Bind off.

Center Band
Cast on 4 sts. Work in St st for 1¼ (1½, 1¾)"/3 (4, 4.5)cm.
Bind off.

Finishing
Wrap the center band around the center of the bow to cinch the middle and sew the cast-on and bound-off edges of center band tog. Thread the button band through the center band. Sew button at end of band, opposite buttonhole. ■

Gauge
20 sts and 32 rows to 4"/10cm over seed stitch using size 7 (4.5mm) needles.
Take time to check gauge.

33
Keyhole Cowl

Choose a lively combination of shades, one solid and one variegated, for this slip-stitch textured cowl.

DESIGNED BY KATHY NORTH

Knitted Measurements
Length 25½"/64.5cm
Width 5¾"/14.5cm

Materials
- 1 3½oz/100g skein (each approx 213yd/195m) of Cascade Yarns *Pacific* (acrylic/superwash merino wool) in #26 Lavender (MC) (4)
- 1 3½oz/100g skein (each approx 213yd/195m) of Cascade Yarns *Pacific Multis* (acrylic/superwash merino wool) in #519 Princess Pastel (CC) (4)
- One pair size 7 (4.5mm) needles, *or size to obtain gauge*
- Two size 7 (4.5mm) double-pointed needles (dpn)
- Size H/8 (5mm) crochet hook for provisional cast-on
- Stitch markers
- Scrap yarn

Provisional Cast-On
Using scrap yarn and crochet hook, ch the number of sts to cast on plus a few extra. Cut a tail and pull the tail through the last chain. With knitting needle and yarn, pick up and knit the stated number of sts through the purl bumps on the back of the chain. To remove scrap-yarn chain, when instructed, pull out the tail from the last crochet stitch. Gently and slowly pull on the tail to unravel the crochet stitches, carefully placing each released knit stitch on a needle.

Slip-Stitch Pattern
(over a multiple of 4 sts plus 3)
Row 1 (WS) With CC, knit.
Row 2 (RS) With MC, k3, *sl 1 wyib, k3; rep from * to end.
Row 3 With MC, k3, *sl 1 wyif, k3; rep from * to end.
Row 4 With CC, k1, *sl 1 wyib, k3; rep from * to last 2 sts, sl 1 wyib, k1.
Row 5 With CC, k1, *sl 1 wyif, k3; rep from * to last 2 sts, sl 1 wyif, k1.
Rep rows 2–5 for slip-stitch pat.

Cowl
With MC, cast on 22 sts using provisional cast-on.
Row 1 (RS) K2, *p2, k2; rep from * to end.
Row 2 (WS) P2, *k2, p2; rep from * to end.
Rep rows 1 and 2 for k2, p2 rib until piece measures 6"/15cm from beg. Slip sts to a dpn. Carefully remove provisional cast-on and place sts on 2nd dpn. With RS of work facing, fold cast-on edge from behind up to sts on last row worked.
Holding needles parallel, work as foll:
Joining row (RS) *K next st on front needle tog with next st on back needle; rep from * to end—22 sts.
Knit 1 row on WS.
Inc row (RS) K3, M1, [k2, M1] 8 times, k3—31 sts.
Knit 1 row on WS. Join CC and knit 1 row.

BEGIN SLIP-STITCH PATTERN
Row 1 (WS) With CC, k2, pm, work row 1 of slip-stitch pat to last 2 sts, pm, k2.
Row 2 (RS) With MC, k2, sm, work row 2 of slip-stitch pat to marker, sm, k2.
Cont to work slip-stitch pat in this way, working 2 sts each side in garter st (ks every row) until slip-stitch section measures 13"/33cm, end with a row 5. Cut CC and cont with MC only to end. With MC, knit 2 rows.
Dec row (RS) K1, k2tog, k10, [k2tog] twice, k10, [k2tog] twice—26 sts.
Knit 1 row, then work in k2, p2 rib for 8"/20.5cm. Bind off in rib.

Finishing
Block lightly to finished measurements. To wear, insert ribbed section through loop. ■

Gauge
22 sts and 36 rows to 4"/10cm over slip-stitch pat using size 7 (4.5mm) needles. *Take time to check gauge.*

34 Checkerboard Blanket

Checkerboards within checkerboards add texture to this cozy blanket, which works up quickly in chunky yarn.

DESIGNED BY LARS RAINS

Knitted Measurements
30 x 31"/76 x 79cm

Materials
- 5 3½oz/100g skeins (each approx 120yd/110m) of Cascade Yarns *Pacific Chunky Color Wave* (acrylic/superwash merino wool) in #403 Tropics (5)
- Size 10½ (6.5mm) circular needle, 32"/80cm long, *or size to obtain gauge*
- Stitch markers

Note
Circular needle is used to accomodate large number of stitches. Do *not* join.

Seed Stitch
(over an even number of sts)
Row 1 (RS) *K1, p1; rep from * to end.
Row 2 K the purl sts and p the knit sts.
Rep row 2 for seed st.

Blanket
Cast on 96 sts.
Work 8 rows in seed st.

BEGIN CHECKERBOARD PATTERN
Row 1 (RS) [K1, p1] 3 times, pm, *k12, [k2, p2] 3 times; rep from * twice more,

k12, pm, [k1, p1] 3 times.
Row 2 Work in seed st to marker, sm, *p12, [k2, p2] 3 times; rep from * twice more, p12, sm, work in seed st to end.
Row 3 Work in seed st to marker, sm, *k12, [p2, k2] 3 times; rep from * twice

more, k12, sm, work in seed st to end.
Row 4 Work in seed st to marker, sm, *p12, [p2, k2] 3 times; rep from * twice more, p12, sm, work in seed st to end.
Rows 5–16 Rep rows 3 and 4 six times more.
Row 17 Work in seed st to marker, sm, *[k2, p2] 3 times, k12; rep from * twice more, [k2, p2] 3 times, sm, work in seed st to end.
Row 18 Work in seed st to marker, sm, *[k2, p2] 3 times, p12; rep from * twice more, [k2, p2] 3 times, sm, work in seed st to end.
Row 19 Work in seed st to marker, sm, *[p2, k2] 3 times, k12; rep from * twice more, [p2, k2] 3 times, sm, work in seed st to end.
Row 20 Work in seed st to marker, sm, *[p2, k2] 3 times, p12; rep from * twice more, [p2, k2] 3 times, sm, work in seed st to end.
Rows 21–32 Rep rows 17–20 three times more.
Rep rows 1–32 three times more, then rep rows 1–16 once more.
Work 8 rows in seed st. Bind off loosely.

Finishing
Block lightly to measurements. ■

Gauge
13 sts and 18 rows to 4"/10cm over St st using size 10½ (6.5mm) needles.
Take time to check gauge.

35 Lace Top

A lovely lace panel dresses up this seed-stitch pullover, adding a unique scalloped shape to the front.

DESIGNED BY CAARIN FLEISCHMANN

Sizes

Instructions are written for sizes 2 (4, 6). Shown in size 6.

Knitted Measurements

Chest 25¾ (29, 31¾)"/65.5 (73.5, 80.5)cm
Back Length 14"/35.5cm
Upper arm 9"/23cm

Materials

- 2 (3, 3) 3½oz/100g skeins (each approx 213yd/195m) of Cascade Yarns *Pacific* (acrylic/superwash merino wool) in #98 Deep Sea Coral (4)
- One pair size 6 (4mm) needles, *or size to obtain gauges*
- 2 stitch markers

Notes

1) Back is wider than front to compensate for the undulation in lace panel.
2) Side seams will pull towards front.
3) Schematic shows front at narrowest width.

Seed Stitch

(over an odd number of sts)
Row 1 (RS) K1, *p1, k1; rep from * to end.
Row 2 K the purl sts and p the knit sts.
Rep row 2 for seed st.

Lace Panel

(worked over 49 sts)
Row 1 and all WS rows Purl.
Rows 2, 6, 10, 14, and 18 K2, [k1, yo] 4 times, [ssk] 3 times, S2KP, [k2tog] 3 times, [yo, k1] 7 times, yo, [ssk] 3 times, S2KP, [k2tog] 3 times, [yo, k1] 4 times, k2.
Rows 4, 8, 12, 16, 20, 24, 28, 32, and 36 Knit.

Rows 22, 26, 30, 34, and 38 K2, [k2tog] 4 times, [yo, k1] 7 times, yo, [ssk] 3 times, S2KP, [k2tog] 3 times, [yo, k1] 7 times, yo, [ssk] 4 times, k2.
Row 40 Knit.
Rep rows 1–40 once more.
Rows 81 and 83 (WS) Purl.
Rows 82 and 84 Knit.

Front

Cast on 63 (71, 75) sts. Knit 3 rows, end with a RS row.

BEGIN LACE PANEL
Row 1 (WS) Work 7 (11, 13) sts in seed st, pm, work row 1 of lace panel over 49 sts, pm, work 7 (11, 13) sts in seed st.
Row 2 Work 7 (11, 13) sts in seed st, sm, work row 2 of lace panel, sm, work 7 (11, 13) sts in seed st.
Cont as established until 55 rows of lace panel have been worked, end with a WS row—side edge measures approx 7½"/19cm.

ARMHOLE SHAPING
Cont to work in pat as established, bind off 4 (4, 6) sts at beg of next 2 rows—55 (63, 63) sts. Cont even until lace panel is complete (84 rows of lace panel worked),

Gauges

17 sts and 35 rows to 4"/10cm over seed st using size 6 (4mm) needles.
49-st Lace panel measures 9"/23cm in width at narrowest width using size 6 (4mm) needles.
Take time to check gauges.

Lace Top

end with a RS row—armhole measures approx 4"/10cm.
Knit 2 rows. Bind off all sts knitwise.

Back
Cast on 57 (63, 71) sts. Knit 2 rows, end with a WS row.
Work in seed st until piece measures 2"/5cm from beg. Place markers at each end of next row and cont in seed st until piece measures 9½"/24cm from beg, end with a WS row.

ARMHOLE SHAPING
Bind off 4 (4, 6) sts at beg of next 2 rows—49 (55, 59) sts.
Cont even in pat until armhole measures 4"/10cm, end with a RS row.
Knit 2 rows. Bind off all sts knitwise.

Sleeves
Cast on 27 sts. Knit 2 rows, end with a WS row.

Work in seed st and work incs as foll:
Work 8 rows even.
Inc 1 st at each side on next row (working inc sts into seed st), then every 8 (10, 10) rows 5 times more—39 sts.
Work even in pat until piece measures 8½ (10, 11)"/21.5 (25.5, 28)cm from beg, end with a WS row.
Knit 2 rows. Bind off all sts knitwise.

Finishing
Block pieces to measurements.
Sew shoulder seams, leaving center 5½ (6, 6)"/14 (15, 15)cm open for neck.
Measure 1 (1, 1½)"/2.5 (2.5, 4)cm down from bound-off edge of sleeve and mark for beg of sleeve cap.
Sew top edge of sleeve cap to straight edge of armhole, then sew side edges of sleeve cap to bound-off sts of armhole.
Sew side and sleeve seams, matching front cast-on edge to markers on back. ■

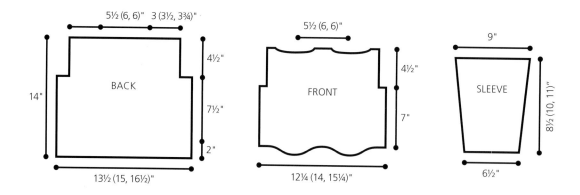

BACK
5½ (6, 6)"   3 (3½, 3¾)"
4½"
7½"
2"
14"
13½ (15, 16½)"

FRONT
5½ (6, 6)"
4½"
7"
12¼ (14, 15¼)"

SLEEVE
9"
8½ (10, 11)"
6½"

Fair Isle Band Cardigan

Fair Isle motifs get graphic on this zip-front cardigan,
which knits up in a jiffy with chunky yarn.

DESIGNED BY AUDREY DRYSDALE

Sizes
Instructions are written for sizes 2 (4, 6).
Shown in size 4.

Knitted Measurements
Chest 24½ (27, 29½)"/62 (68.5, 75)cm
Length 13 (14, 15½)"/33 (35.5, 37.5)cm
Upper arm 10 (10, 10½)"/25.5 (25.5, 26.5)cm

Materials
■ 3 (3, 4) 3½oz/100g skeins (each
approx 120yd/110m) of Cascade Yarns
Pacific Chunky (acrylic/superwash merino
wool) in #62 Charcoal (A) (**5**)
■ 1 skein each in #94 Jet Heather (B),
#61 Silver (C), and #02 White (D)
■ One each sizes 9 and 10 (5.5 and
6mm) circular needle, 24"/60cm long,
or size to obtain gauge
■ Stitch markers
■ Stitch holders
■ One 12 (12,14)"/30 (30, 36)cm
separating zipper
■ Matching sewing thread

K1, P1 Rib
(over an odd number of sts)
Row 1 (RS) K1, *p1, k1; rep from * to end.
Row 2 P1, *k1, p1; rep from * to end.
Rep rows 1 and 2 for k1, p1 rib.

Note
Circular needles are used to accommodate
large number of stitches. Do *not* join.

Body
With smaller needle and A, cast on 89
(99, 109) sts. Working back and forth in
rows, work in k1, p1 rib for 6 rows, inc
2 sts evenly across the last WS row—91
(101,111) sts.

Change to larger needle.
Knit 1 row, purl 1 row.

BEGIN CHART 1
Row 1 (RS) Beg with st 6 (1, 6) of chart,
work to end of rep line, then work the
20-st rep for 3 (4, 4) reps more, then
work sts 2–16 (0, 2–16). Cont to foll
chart in this way through row 11.
Cont in St st (k on RS, p on WS) with A
only until piece measures 8 (9, 10)"/20.5
(23, 25.5)cm from beg.

DIVIDE FOR FRONT AND BACK
Next row (RS) K21 (23, 26) for right
front and place sts on holder, bind off 4
sts, k until there are 41 (47, 51) sts on
needle for back and place sts on holder,
bind off 4 sts, k to end for left front.

Left Front
Cont on the 21 (23, 26) left front sts
only, work as foll:
Next row (WS) Purl.
Dec row 1 K1, k2tog, k to end—20 (22,
25) sts.

For size 2 only
Next row (WS) Purl.

Gauge
15 sts and 19 rows to 4"/10 cm over St st using larger needle. *Take time to check gauge*

Fair Isle Band Cardigan

For sizes 4 and 6 only
Dec row 2 (WS) P to last 3 sts, p2tog, p1—(21, 24) sts.

For size 6 only
Next 3 rows Rep dec rows 1, 2, and 1—21 sts.
Next row (WS) Purl.

Cont as foll for all sizes

BEGIN CHART 2
Row 1 (RS) With A, k1, k2tog 0 (1, 1) times, k to end (counts as chart row 1)—20 sts. Cont to foll chart 2 through row 8, working decs at beg of RS rows—17 sts. Working with A only, cont to shape armhole by dec 1 st at beg of every RS row twice more—15 sts. Purl 1 row.

NECK SHAPING
Next row (RS) K1, k2tog, k6, bind off next 6 sts. Cut A.
Next row (WS) Rejoin A to neck edge, p2tog, p6—7 sts.
Dec row K1, k2tog, k2, k2tog—5 sts.
Dec row P2tog, p3—4 sts.
Dec row K1, k2tog, k1—3 sts.
Next row Purl.
Dec row K1, k2tog—2 sts.
Next row Purl.
Next row K2tog. Fasten off last st.

Right Front
Transfer the 21 (23, 26) right front sts from holder to needle ready to work a WS row, and work armhole shaping as foll:
Next row (WS) Purl.
Dec row 1 (RS) K to last 3 sts, ssk, k1—20 (22, 25) sts.

For size 2 only
Next row (WS) Purl.

For sizes 4 and 6 only
Dec row 2 (WS) P1, p2tog tbl, p to end of row—(21, 24) sts.

For size 6 only
Next 3 rows Rep dec rows 1, 2, and 1—21 sts.
Next row (WS) Purl.

Cont as foll for all sizes

BEGIN CHART 3
Row 1 (RS) With A, k to the last 3 sts, ssk 0 (1, 1) times, k to end—20 sts. Cont to foll chart 3 through row 8, working decs at end of RS rows—17 sts. Working with A only, cont to shape armhole by dec 1 st at end of every RS row twice more—15 sts. Purl 1 row.

NECK SHAPING
Next row (RS) Bind off 6 sts, k to last 3 sts, ssk, k1.
Next row (WS) P6, p2tog—7 sts.
Dec row K2tog, k2, ssk, k1—5 sts.
Dec row P3, p2tog—4 sts.
Dec row K1, ssk, k1—3 sts.
Next row Purl.
Dec row Ssk, k1—2 sts.
Next row Purl.
Next row Ssk. Fasten off last st.

Back
Rejoin A to the 41 (47, 51) sts for back, ready to work a WS row.
Next row (WS) Purl.
Dec row 1 (RS) K1, k2tog 0 (1, 1) times, k to last 3 sts, ssk 0 (1, 1) times, k to end—41 (45, 49) sts.

For size 2 only
Next row (WS) Purl.

For sizes 4 and 6 only
Dec row 2 (WS) P1, p2tog tbl, p to the last 3 sts, p2tog, p1—(43, 47) sts.

For size 6 only
Next 3 rows Rep dec row 1 on the foll 2 RS rows—43 sts.

Cont as foll for all sizes

BEGIN CHART 4
Row 1 (RS) With A, k1, k2tog 0 (1, 1)

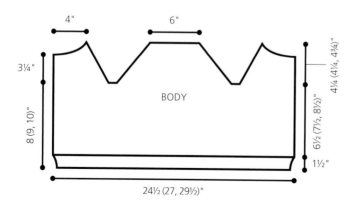

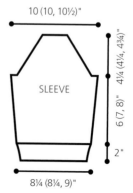

36

Fair Isle Band Cardigan

times, k to last 3 sts, ssk 0 (1, 1) times, k to end—41 sts.

Foll chart, cont to shape armhole by dec 1 st each side of every RS row 3 times more—35 sts.

Working with A only, cont to shape armhole, dec every RS row until 17 sts rem. Purl 1 row. Bind off.

Sleeves

With smaller needle and A, cast on 29 (29, 31) sts. Work in k1, p1 rib for 8 rows, inc 2 sts evenly across the last WS row—31 (31, 33) sts.

Change to larger needle; with A only, knit 1 rnd, purl 1 rnd.

BEGIN CHART 5

Row 1 (RS) K0 (0, 1) with A, then foll chart for the 31 sts, k0 (0, 1) with A. Cont to foll chart 5 through row 11 in this way, inc 1 st each side on row 7. Then cont with A only and inc 1 st each side every 8th row twice more —37 (37, 39) sts. Work even until piece measures 8 (9, 10)"/20.5 (23, 25.5)cm from beg.

RAGLAN CAP SHAPING

Bind off 2 sts at beg of next 2 rows.

Dec row 1 (RS) K1, k2tog, k to last 3 sts, ssk, k1—2 sts dec'd.

Dec row 2 (WS) P1, p2tog tbl, p to last 3 sts, p2tog, p1—2 sts dec'd.

For size 6 only

Rep dec row 1 on next RS row. Work 3 rows even—29 sts for all sizes.

BEGIN CHART 4

Work the 8 rows of chart 4, dec 1 st each side as on dec row 1 on chart rows 1, 3, 5, and 7. Then, working with A only, rep dec row 1 every RS row 6 times more—9 sts. If necessary, work even until there are same number of rows as back. Bind off.

Collar

With smaller needle and A, cast on 4 sts.

Row 1 (WS) Knit.

Next row (RS) Kfb, k to last 2 sts, kfb, k1.

Next row Knit.

Rep the last 2 rows 3 times more—12 sts.

Next row (RS) Kfb, k to end.

Next row (WS) Knit.

Rep the last 2 rows 3 times more—16 sts. Place marker at end of the last row worked. Work even in garter st (knit every row) until piece measures 6½"/16.5cm from the marker.

Next row (RS) K2tog, k to end.

Next row (WS) Knit.

Rep the last 2 rows 3 times more—12 sts.
Next row K2tog, k to last 2 sts, k2tog.
Next row Knit.
Rep the last 2 rows 3 times more—4
sts. Bind off.

Finishing
Block pieces to measurements.
Sew raglan sleeves into raglan
armholes. Sew sleeve seams.

FRONT TRIM
With RS facing, smaller needles, and
A, beg at lower right front edge,
pick up and k 40 (45, 50) sts along
right front edge to neck. Knit 2
rows. Bind off.
Work left front trim to correspond.

Pm at center back neck edge and at
center collar edge. Center the collar
and pin or baste in place. Sew collar
to neck edges.

ZIPPER
Pin, then baste, the zipper in place
along the center front. Sew zipper in
place with thread, using one row of
backstitch next to the zipper teeth
and one row of whipstitch along
the outer edge of the zipper tape to
hold in place. ∎

CHART 5 — SLEEVES

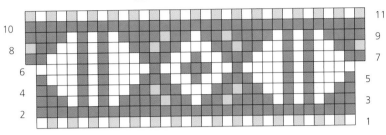

31 sts

CHART 4 — BACK/SLEEVES

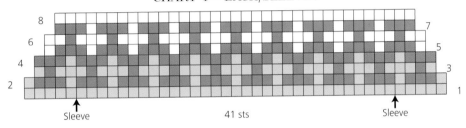

Sleeve   41 sts   Sleeve

CHART 3 — RIGHT FRONT

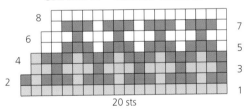

20 sts

CHART 1 — BODY

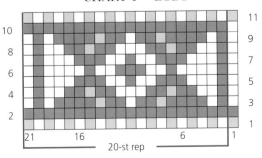

21   16   6   1
20-st rep

CHART 2 — LEFT FRONT

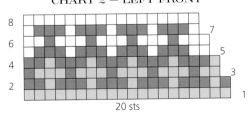

20 sts

COLOR KEY

B
C
D

105

V-Neck Vest

A textured chevron pattern livens up this classic sweater vest.

DESIGNED BY KIRI FITZGERALD-HILLIER

Sizes
Instructions are written for sizes 2 (4, 6). Shown in size 4.

Knitted Measurements
Chest 22½ (25, 28)"/57 (63.5, 71)cm
Length 14½ (15½, 16½)"/37 (39.5, 42)cm

Materials
- 2 (2, 3) 3½oz/100g skeins (each approx 213yd/195m) of Cascade Yarns *Pacific* (acrylic/superwash merino wool) in #09 Sand (A) (4)
- 1 skein in #96 Treetop (B)
- One each sizes 6 and 7 (4 and 4.5mm) circular needle, 24"/61cm long, *or size to obtain gauge*
- Size 6 (4mm) circular needle, 16"/41cm long
- Spare size 7 (4.5mm) circular needle, 24"/61cm long
- One pair size 7 (4.5mm) needles
- One set (5) size 6 (4mm) double-pointed needles (dpn)
- Stitch holder
- Stitch markers

Notes
1) Body is worked in one piece to the underarms.
2) To work in the rnd, always read chart from right to left.

Body
With B and smaller, longer circular needle, cast on 110 (125, 140) sts. Join, taking care not to twist sts, and pm for beg of rnd. Work in k2, p3 rib for 8 rnds. Change to larger circular needle and A.
Inc rnd Knit, inc 2 (1, 0) sts evenly spaced—112 (126, 140) sts.
Work even in St st (k every rnd) until piece measures 2 (2½, 3)"/5 (6.5, 7.5)cm from beg.

BEGIN CHART
Rnd 1 Work 14-st rep 8 (9, 10) times around.
Cont to foll chart in this way to rnd 28.
Inc rnd Knit, inc 1 (0, 1) st at beg of rnd—113 (126, 141) sts.
Cont to work even in St st until piece measures 8 (8½, 9)"/20.5 (21.5, 23)cm from beg.

BEGIN V-NECK SHAPING
Next rnd K84 (94, 104), bind off next st, k28 (31, 36)—112 (125, 140) sts.
Next row K to bound-off st, turn. Using spare circular needle, work back and forth in rows as foll:
Next row (WS) Purl.

Dec row (RS) K1, ssk, k to last 3 sts, k2tog, k1—110 (123, 138) sts.
Next row Purl.
Rep last 2 rows twice more—106 (119, 134) sts. Piece measures approx 9½ (10, 10½)"/24 (25.5, 26.5)cm from beg.

DIVIDE FOR FRONT AND BACK
Cont to shape neck and divide sts as foll:
Next row (RS) K1, ssk, k19 (21, 24), bind off next 6 (8, 10) sts, k until there are 50 (55, 60) sts on RH needle, bind off next 6 (8, 10) sts, k to last 3 sts, k2tog, k1—21 (23, 26) sts for right front; 50 (55, 60) sts for back; 21 (23, 26) sts for left front.
Hold sts on circular needle until needed.

Left Front
Using straight needles, shape armhole and cont neck shaping as foll:
Row 1 (WS) Purl
Dec row 2 (RS) Bind off 2 sts, k to last 3 sts, k2tog, k1—18 (20, 23) sts.
Row 3 Purl.
Dec row 4 Bind off 1 st, k to last 3 sts, k2tog, k1—16 (18, 21) sts.
Row 5 Purl.
Dec row 6 Bind off 1 st, k to last 3 sts, k2tog, k1—14 (16, 19) sts.
Row 7 Purl.

Gauge
20 sts and 26 rnds to 4"/10cm over St st using larger needles.
Take time to check gauge.

V-Neck Vest

Dec row 8 K to last 3 sts, k2tog, k1—13 (15, 18) sts.
Rep rows 7 and 8 for 5 (6, 7) times more—8 (9, 11) sts. Work even until armhole measures 4½ (5, 5½)"/11.5 (12.5, 14)cm, end with a WS row.

SHOULDER SHAPING
At armhole edge, bind off 4 (4, 5) sts once, then 4 (5, 6) sts once.

Right Front
Place 21 (23, 26) sts on straight needle ready to work a WS row. Shape armhole and cont neck shaping as foll:
Row 1 (WS) Bind off 2 sts, p to end—19 (21, 24) sts.
Row 2 (RS) K1, ssk, k to end—18 (20, 23) sts.
Row 3 Bind off 1 st, p to end—17 (19, 22) sts.
Row 4 K1, ssk, k to end—16 (18, 21) sts.
Row 5 Bind off 1 st, p to end—15 (17, 20) sts.
Row 6 K1, ssk, k to end—14 (16, 19) sts.
Row 7 Purl.
Rep rows 6 and 7 for 6 (7, 8) times more—8 (9, 11) sts.
Work even until armhole measures same as left front to shoulder, end with a RS row.

SHOULDER SHAPING
At armhole edge, bind off 4 (4, 5) sts once, then 4 (5, 6) sts once.

Back
Place 50 (55, 60) sts on straight needle ready to work a WS row.

ARMHOLE SHAPING
Bind off 2 sts at beg of next 2 rows, then 1 st at beg of next 4 rows.
Work even on 42 (47, 52) sts until

armhole measures same length as left front to shoulder, end with a WS row.

SHOULDER SHAPING
Bind off 4 (4, 5) sts at beg of next 2 rows, then 4 (5, 6) sts at beg of next 2 rows. Place rem 26 (29, 30) sts on holder for back neck.

Finishing
Block piece to measurements.
Sew shoulder seams.

NECKBAND
With RS facing, smaller, shorter circular needle, and B, k26 (29, 30) sts from back neck holder, pick up and k 34 (36, 40) sts evenly spaced along left front edge, pm, pick up and k 1 in bound-off st, pick up

and k 30 (35, 40) sts evenly spaced along right front edge—91 (101, 111) sts. Join and pm for beg of rnd.
Rnd 1 Work k2, p3 rib to 5 sts before marker, k2, p1, k2tog, sm, k1, ssk, p1, k2, work p3, k2 rib to last 3 sts, end p3.
Rnd 2 Work in rib as established to 2 sts before marker, k2tog, sm, k1, ssk, work in rib to end.
Rep rnd 2 six times more.
Bind off loosely in rib.

ARMBANDS
With RS facing, dpn, and B, pick up and k 65 (70, 75) sts evenly spaced around armhole edge, dividing sts evenly over 4 dpn as you go. Join and pm for beg of rnd. Work around in k2, p3 rib for 8 rnds. Bind off loosely in rib. ■

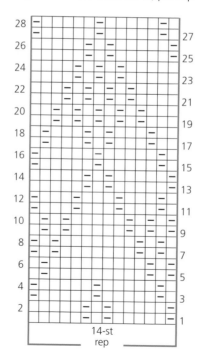

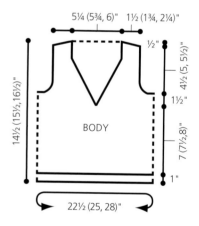

5¼ (5¾, 6)" 1½ (1¾, 2¼)"

½"

4½ (5, 5½)"

1½"

BODY

7 (7½, 8)"

1"

14½ (15½, 16½)"

22½ (25, 28)"

STITCH KEY
☐ k on RS, p on WS
⊟ p on RS, k on WS

38

Icelandic Pullover

This bright, colorful sweater features a circular yoke
and is worked seamlessly in the round.

DESIGNED BY LARS RAINS

Sizes
Instructions are written for sizes 2 (4, 6).
Shown in size 4.

Knitted Measurements
Chest 24½ (26, 28)"/62 (66, 71)cm
Length 13 (14, 15)"/33 (35.5, 38)cm
Upper arm 9¾ (10½, 11½)"/24.5 (26.5, 29)cm

Materials
■ 3 (3, 4) 3½oz/100g skeins (each
approx 120yd/110m) of Cascade Yarns
Pacific Chunky (acrylic/superwash merino
wool) in #24 Platinum (MC) (5)
■ 1 skein each in #103 Deep Teal (A),
#84 Persimmon (B), and #95 Lime Green (C)
■ One each sizes 9 and 10½ (5.5 and
6.5mm) circular needle, 24"/60cm long,
or size to obtain gauge
■ One size 10½ (6.5mm) circular needle,
16"/40cm long
■ One set (5) each sizes 9 and 10½ (5.5
and 6.5mm) double-pointed needles (dpn)
■ Stitch holders
■ Stitch marker

Note
When working chart pat, read all rows of
chart from right to left.

Stitch Glossary
M1R (make 1 right) Insert left needle
from *back to front* into the horizontal
strand between the last st worked and
the next st on left needle, knit this strand
through the front loop to twist the st.

M1L (make 1 left) Insert left needle
from *front to back* into the horizontal
strand between the last st worked and
the next st on left needle, knit this strand
through the back loop to twist the st.

Sleeves
With smaller dpn and A, cast on 20 (20,
24) sts and divide sts evenly over 4 dpn.
Join, taking care not to twist sts, and pm
for beg of rnd.
Change to MC.
Work in k2, p2 rib for 6 rnds.
Change to larger dpn and St st (k every
rnd).
Work even for 4 (4, 6) rnds.
Inc rnd K1, M1L, k to 1 st before marker,
M1R, k1.
Rep inc rnd every 6th rnd 5 (6, 6) times
more—32 (34, 38) sts.
Work even until piece measures 9½
(11½, 12½)"/24 (29, 31.5)cm from beg,
end 3 (3, 4) sts before rnd marker.
Next rnd K6 (6, 8) dropping marker,
place these 6 (6, 8) sts on a length of
yarn for underarm, k to end of rnd.
Place rem 26 (28, 30) sts on holder for
sleeve. Set aside.

Gauge
13 sts and 18 rnds to 4"/10cm over St st using larger needles. *Take time to check gauge.*

Icelandic Pullover

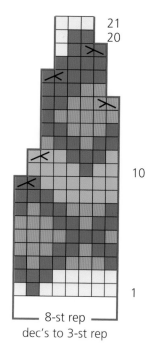

Body

With smaller circular needle and A, cast on 80 (84, 92) sts. Join, taking care not to twist sts, and pm for beg of rnd. Change to MC. Work in k2, p2 rib for 6 rnds.

Change to longer, larger circular needle and St st.

Work even until piece measures 7 (7½, 8)"/18 (19, 20.5)cm from beg, end 3 (3, 4) sts before marker.

Next rnd K6 (6, 8) dropping marker, place these 6 (6, 8) sts on a st holder for left underarm, k until there are 34 (36, 38) sts on RH needle (front), k6 (6, 8), place these 6 (6, 8) sts on a st holder for right underarm, k rem 34 (36, 38) sts (back)—68 (72, 76) sts.

Yoke

Join sleeves and body on larger, longer circular needle with MC as foll:

Next rnd K26 (28, 30) sleeve sts, k 34 (36, 38) front sts, k26 (28, 30) sleeve sts, k34 (36, 38) back sts—120 (128, 136) sts. Join and pm for beg of rnd.

Cont in St st, work even for 1 (4, 6) rnds.

BEGIN CHART PATTERN

Rnd 1 Work 8-st rep 15 (16, 17) times. Cont to foll chart in this way to rnd 21, changing to shorter, larger needle when needed—45 (48, 51) sts. Change to larger dpn, dividing sts evenly over 4 needles, and work to end with MC as foll:

Dec rnd K0 (0, 1), *k3 (k2, k3), k2tog; rep from * around—36 (36, 41) sts.

For sizes 2 and 4 only
Next rnd Knit.

For size 6 only
Dec rnd K2tog, k to end—40 sts.

For all sizes

NECKBAND

Change to smaller dpn. Work in k2, p2 rib for 6 rnds. Bind off loosely in rib.

Finishing

Block piece to measurements. Graft underarm sts using Kitchener stitch. ■

— 8-st rep —
dec's to 3-st rep

COLOR KEY

☐	MC	▨	B
▦	A	▨	C

STITCH KEY

☐ k with color indicated

◿ k2tog with color indicated

◺ ssk with color indicated

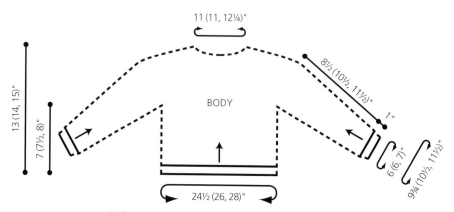

39

Short-Row Scarf

Short rows give this scarf a soft curve,
and a contrasting picot bind-off gives it a fancy edge.

DESIGNED BY MATTHEW SCHRANK

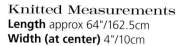

Knitted Measurements
Length approx 64"/162.5cm
Width (at center) 4"/10cm

Materials
▪ 1 3½oz/100g skein (each approx 213yd/195m) of Cascade Yarns *Pacific Multi*s (acrylic/superwash merino wool) in #532 Roses (A) (4)
▪ 1 3½oz/100g skein (each approx 213yd/195m) of Cascade Yarns *Pacific* (acrylic/superwash merino wool) in #106 Carmine Rose (B) (4)
▪ One size 7 (4.5mm) needle, *or size to obtain gauge*

Scarf
With A, cast on 250 sts.
Rows 1 and 2 Knit all sts.
Short row 3 K to last st, turn work.
Short row 4 K to last st, turn work.
Rows 5–12 Rep rows 1–4 twice more.
Short rows 13 and 14 Rep short rows 3 and 4 once more.
Short row 15 K to last 2 sts, turn work.

Short row 16 K to last 2 sts, turn work.
Short rows 17–20 Rep short rows 15 and 16 twice more.
Short row 21 K to last 3 sts, turn work.
Short row 22 K to last 3 sts, turn work.
Short rows 23 and 24 Rep short rows 21 and 22 once more.
Short row 25 K to last 4 sts, turn work.
Short row 26 K to last 4 sts, turn work.
Short rows 27 and 28 Rep short rows 25 and 26 once more.
Short row 29 K to last 5 sts, turn work.
Short row 30 K to last 5 sts, turn work.
Short rows 31 and 32 Rep short rows 29 and 30 once more.
Row 33 K to end of row.
Row 34 K to end of row.
Change to B.
Knit 2 rows.

PICOT BIND-OFF
With B, *cast on 2 sts, k2, pass 2nd st over first st to bind off 1 st, bind off next 3 sts, sl rem st on RH needle back to LH needle; rep from * until all sts are bound off.

Finishing
Weave in ends. Block to measurements. ▪

Gauge
20 sts and 36 rows to 4"/10cm over garter st using size 7 (4.5mm) needles.
Take time to check gauge.

Poncho

This stylish little topper is created with two lace rectangles that are seamed into a perfect poncho shape.

DESIGNED BY DORCAS LAVERY

Knitted Measurements
Width (edge to edge) 21"/53.5cm
Length 18"/45.5cm

Materials
- 4 3½oz/100g skeins (each approx 213yd/195m) of Cascade Yarns *Pacific Color Wave* (acrylic/superwash merino wool) in #326 Sunrise (4)
- One pair size 9 (5.5mm) needles, *or size to obtain gauge*
- Stitch markers

Notes
1) Poncho is constructed with 2 identical rectangles sewn to form poncho shape.
2) Stitch count varies within lace pattern and returns to original count after row 8 is completed.

Rectangles
Loosely cast on 55 sts.
Rows 1–3 Knit.
Row 4 K5, pm, k46, pm, k4.
Row 5 K4, sm, p to marker while dec 3 sts evenly across, sm, k5—52 sts.
Row 6 K5, sm, *k2, yo; rep from * to 1 st before marker, k1, sm, k4.
Row 7 K4, p to marker, k5.
Row 8 K5, sm, k1, *yo, S2KP; rep from * to marker, sm, k4—52 sts.
Row 9 Rep row 7.
Rep rows 6–9 until piece measures 19"/48cm from beg.
Next row K across while inc 3 sts evenly between markers—55 sts.
Knit 3 rows. Loosely bind off.

Finishing
Block rectangles to 10x20"/25.5x51cm. Place marker at right edge of first triangle 10"/25.5cm from cast-on edge. Sew bound-off edge of second triangle between cast-on edge and marker. Place marker at right edge of second triangle 10"/25.5cm from cast-on edge. Sew bound-off edge of first triangle between cast-on edge and marker. ■

Gauge
19 sts and 28 rows to 4"/10cm over lace pat using size 9 (5.5mm) needles.
Take time to check gauge.

Fair Isle Cardi

This sweetheart of a sweater is worked seamlessly,
then fastened at the top with a single large button.

DESIGNED BY CHERYL MURRAY

Sizes
Instructions are written for sizes 2 (4, 6).
Shown in size 4.

Knitted Measurements
Chest (closed) 26 (28, 30)"/66 (71, 76)cm
Length 13½ (14½, 15½)"/34 (37, 39.5)cm
Upper arm 11 (12, 13)"/28 (30.5, 33)cm

Materials
- 2 (2, 3) 3½oz/100g skeins (each
approx 213yd/195m) of Cascade Yarns
Pacific (acrylic/superwash merino wool) in
#02 White (A) 🔵
- 1 skein each in #106 Carmine Rose (B),
#95 Lime Green (C), and #61 Silver (D)
- One each sizes 6 and 7 (4 and 4.5mm)
circular needles, 24"/41cm long,
or size to obtain gauge
- One pair size 7 (4.5mm) needles
- One set (5) each sizes 6 and 7 (4 and
4.5mm) double-pointed needles (dpn)
- Stitch holders
- Stitch marker
- One 1"/25mm button

Notes
1) Body is worked in one piece to the
underarms.
2) Circular needles are used on the body
to accommodate the larger number of sts.
Do *not* join. Work back and forth in rows.
3) Sleeves are worked in the round using dpn.

3-Needle Bind-Off
1) Divide sts evenly between two needles
and hold RS together.
2) Insert third needle knitwise into first
st on each needle and knit these two sts
together, dropping them from the LH
needles. *Knit the next two sts together
in the same manner.
3) Pass first st on third needle over second
st and off needle. Rep from * in step 2
across row until all sts are bound off.

K1, P1 Rib
(over a multiple of 2 sts plus 1)
Row 1 (RS) K1, *p1, k1; rep from * to end.
Row 2 P1, *k1, p1; rep from * to end.
Rep rows 1 and 2 for k1, p1 rib.

Body
With smaller circular needle and A, cast on
145 (157, 169) sts. Do *not* join. Work back
and forth in k1, p1 rib for 10 rows, end with
a WS row. Change to larger circular needle.

BEGIN CHART PATTERN
Row 1 (RS) Work first st, work 12-st rep
12 (13, 14) times.
Row 2 Work 12-st rep 12 (13, 14) times,
work last st.

Gauge
23 sts and 26 rows to 4"/10cm over St st and chart pat using larger needles.
Take time to check gauge.

Fair Isle Cardi

Cont to foll chart in this way through row 37, then rep rows 31–37 until piece measures 8 (8½, 9)"/20.5 (21.5, 23)cm from beg, end with a WS row.

DIVIDE FOR FRONTS AND BACK
Next row (RS) Work across first 34 (37, 40) sts, place these sts on holder for right front, bind off next 2 sts for right underarm, work until there are 73 (79, 85) sts on RH needle, leave these sts on needle for back, bind off next 2 sts for left underarm, work to end, place these last 34 (37, 40) sts on holder for left front.

Back
Change to straight needles. Cont in chart pat as established until armhole measures 5½ (6, 6½)"/14 (15, 16.5)cm, end with a WS row.

SHOULDERS AND BACK NECK SHAPING
Next row (RS) With D, work first 21 (23, 25) sts, place these sts on holder for right back shoulder, bind off next 31 (33, 35) sts for back neck, work last 21 (23, 25) sts, place these sts on holder for left back shoulder.

Left Front
Place 34 (37, 40) sts from left front holder onto larger straight needles ready for a WS row. Cont in chart pat as established until armhole measures 3 (3½, 4)"/7.5 (9, 10)cm, end with a RS row.

NECK SHAPING
Bind off 7 (8, 9) sts at beg of next row. Dec 1 st from neck edge on next row, then every other row 5 times more. Work even on 21 (23, 25) sts until piece measures same length as back to shoulder, end with a WS row. With D, k21 (23, 25), place these sts on holder for left front shoulder.

Right Front
Place 34 (37, 40) sts from right front holder onto larger straight needles ready for a WS row. Cont in chart pat as established until armhole measures 3 (3½, 4)"/7.5 (9, 10)cm, end with a WS row.

NECK SHAPING
Bind off 7 (8, 9) sts at beg of next row. Dec 1 st from neck edge on next row, then every other row 5 times more. Work even on 21 (23, 25) sts until piece measures same length as back to shoulder, end with a WS row. With D, k 21 (23, 25) sts, place these sts on holder for right front shoulder. Using larger dpn and D, join front and back shoulders using 3-needle bind-off.

Sleeves
With RS of armhole facing, larger dpn, and A, dividing sts evenly over 4 needles as you go, pick up and k 1 st in 2nd bound-off st of armhole, 31 (34, 37) sts evenly spaced to shoulder seam, 31 (34, 37) sts evenly spaced to bottom of armhole, and 1 st in first bound-off st of armhole—64 (70, 76) sts. Join and pm for beg of rnd.
Work 1 rnd even in St st (k every rnd).
Dec rnd K1, ssk, k to 3 sts before marker, k2tog, k1.
Rep dec rnd every other rnd 5 times more, then every 4th rnd 7 (9, 11) times—38 (40, 42) sts.
Work even until piece measures 6 (7, 8)"/15 (18, 20.5)cm from beg.
Change to smaller dpn. Work 10 rnds in k1, p1 rib. Bind off loosely in rib.

Finishing
Weave in ends and block piece to measurements.

NECKBAND
With RS facing, smaller circular needle, and A, pick up and k 65 (69, 73) sts evenly spaced along neck edge.
Work in k1, p1 rib for 8 rows.
Bind off loosely in rib.

BUTTONBAND
With RS facing, smaller circular needle, and A, pick up and k 61 (67, 73) sts

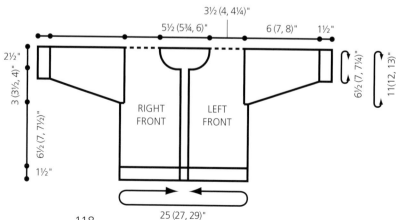

evenly spaced along left front edge.
Work in k1, p1 rib for 10 rows.
Bind off loosely in rib.

BUTTONHOLE BAND

With RS facing, smaller circular needle
and A, pick up and k 61 (67, 73) sts
evenly spaced along right front edge.
Work in k1, p1 rib for 5 rows, end with a
WS row.
Buttonhole row (RS) Work in rib to last
9 sts, bind off next 3 sts, work in rib to end.
Next row Work in rib, casting on 3 sts
over bound-off sts.
Cont in rib for 3 rows more.
Bind off loosely in rib.
Sew button opposite buttonhole. ■

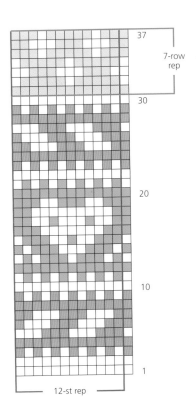

37

7-row
rep

30

20

10

1

12-st rep

COLOR KEY

☐ A ▦ C

▨ B ▨ D

Pumpkin Hat

Worked seamlessly in the round, this hat is a perfect pick for keeping little cutie pies warm on chilly autumn days.

DESIGNED BY KATHY NORTH

Knitted Measurements
Brim circumference (unstretched)
14"/35.5cm
Height 8½"/21.5cm

Materials
■ 1 3½oz/100g skein (each approx 213yd/195m) of Cascade Yarns *Pacific* (acrylic/superwash merino wool) each in #84 Persimmon (A) and #56 Kelly Green (B) (4)
■ One each sizes 6 and 8 (4 and 5mm) circular needle, 16"/40cm long, *or size to obtain gauges*
■ One set (5) size 8 (5mm) double-pointed needles (dpn)
■ Stitch marker
■ Tapestry needle

Note
Hat will stretch to fit most.

Hat
With smaller circular needle and B, cast on 72 sts loosely. Join, being careful to not twist sts, and pm for beg of rnd.

BRIM
Rnds 1–4 Knit.
Rnds 5–15 *K2, p2; rep from * around.
Rnd 16 Knit.
Cut B, leaving tail for weaving in later.

BODY
Rnd 17 With A, knit.
Change to larger circular needle.
Inc rnd 18 *K3, M1; rep from * around—96 sts.
Rnd 19 Knit.
Rnd 20 K4, p4, *k8, p4; rep from * to last 4 sts, k4.
Inc rnd 21 K3, M1, k1, p4, *k1, M1, k6, M1, k1, p4; rep from * to last 4 sts, k1, M1, k3—112 sts.
Rnd 22 K5, p4, *k10, p4; rep from * to last 5 sts, k5.
Rep rnd 22 until piece measures 8"/20.5cm from beg.

SHAPE CROWN
Note Change to dpn when sts no longer fit comfortably on circular needle.
Dec rnd 1 K2, k2tog, k1, [p2tog] twice, *k1, ssk, k4, k2tog, k1, [p2tog] twice; rep from * to last 5 sts, k1, ssk, k2—80 sts.
Rnd 2 K4, p2, *k8, p2; rep from * to last 4 sts, k4.

Dec rnd 3 K1, k2tog, k1, p2, *k1, ssk, k2, k2tog, k1, p2; rep from * to last 4 sts, k1, ssk, k1—64 sts.
Rnd 4 K3, p2, *k6, p2; rep from * to last 3 sts, k3.
Dec rnd 5 K1, k2tog, p2tog, *k1, ssk, k2tog, k1, p2tog; rep from * to last 3 sts, k1, ssk— 40 sts.
Rnd 6 K2, p1, *k4, p1; rep from * to last 2 sts, k2.
Dec rnd 7 K2tog, p1, *ssk, k2tog, p1; rep from * to last 2 sts, ssk—24 sts.
Rnd 8 K1, p1,*k2, p1; rep from * to last st, k1.
Dec rnd 9 *K2tog; rep from * around—12 sts.
Rep dec rnd 9 twice more—3 sts.
Cut A, leaving tail for weaving in later.
With B, work I-cord as foll:
***Row 1 (RS)** K3, do *not* turn work. Slide sts to beg of needle to work next row from RS. Pull yarn tightly from the end of the row. Rep from * until I-cord measures approx 3"/7.5cm. Bind off.

Finishing
Weave in ends. Block crown of hat over a small plate. ■

20 sts and 25 rnds to 4"/10cm over St st using larger needles.
20 sts and 26 rnds to 4"/10cm over k2, p2 rib (unstretched) using smaller needles. *Take time to check gauges.*

Cabled Pullover

With its squishy cables and garter-stitch sleeves,
this sweater has plenty of interest for knitters and plenty of texture for little hands.

DESIGNED BY CAARIN FLEISCHMANN

Sizes
Instructions are written for sizes 2 (4, 6). Shown in size 4.

Knitted Measurements
Chest 25 (26, 29)"/63.5 (66, 73.5)cm
Length 14¾ (16½, 18¼)"/37.5 (42, 46.5)cm
Upper arm 9 (9½, 10½)"/23 (24, 26.5)cm

Materials
- 3 (4, 4) 3½oz/100g skeins (each approx 213yd/195m) of Cascade Yarns *Pacific* (acrylic/superwash merino wool) in #85 Cobalt (⁴)
- One each sizes 5 and 6 (3.75 and 4mm) circular needles, 24"/60cm long, *or size to obtain gauges*
- One set (5) each sizes 5 and 6 (3.75 and 4mm) double-pointed needles (dpn)
- Cable needle (cn)
- Stitch markers
- Stitch holders

Notes
1) Body and sleeves are worked in the rnd separately and joined for working the yoke.
2) Yoke is worked in the rnd to front neck shaping, then worked back and forth in rows.
3) When decreasing in cable pat, if there are not enough sts to cross cables, knit sts instead.
4) When working back and forth in cable pat, all odd-numbered (WS) rows are purled.
5) When working back and forth in garter st, all odd-numbered (WS) rows are knit.

Stitch Glossary
6-st RC Sl 3 to cn and hold to *back*, k3, k3 from cn.
6-st LC Sl 3 to cn and hold to *front*, k3, k3 from cn.

Cable Pattern
(over a multiple of 9 sts)
Rnd 1 *K3, 6-st RC; rep from * around.
Rnds 2–4 Knit.
Rnd 5 *6-st LC, k3; rep from * around.
Rnds 6–8 Knit.
Rep rnds 1–8 for cable pat.

Twisted Rib
(over an even number of sts)
Rnd 1 *K1 tbl, p1 tbl; rep from * around.
Rep rnd 1 for twisted rib.

Sleeves
With larger dpn, cast on 28 (28, 30) sts.
Divide sts evenly between 4 dpn. Join and pm for beg of rnd.
Work 10 rnds in garter st (knit 1 rnd, purl 1 rnd).
Inc rnd K1, M1, kto last st, M1, k1—30 (30, 32) sts.
Cont in garter st, working inc rnd every 8th (10th, 10th) rnd 6 (7, 8) times more—42 (44, 48) sts.
Work even until piece measures 8½ (10, 11½)"/21.5 (25.5, 29)cm from beg, end on a purl rnd and 3 (3, 4) sts before beg-of-rnd marker.
Next rnd P3 (3, 4), k3 (3, 4) and place these 6 (6, 8) sts on st holder, removing marker, k to end. Place rem 36 (38, 40) sts on st holder. Set aside.

Body
With smaller circular needle, cast on 130 (136, 152) sts. Join, being careful not to twist sts, and pm for beg of rnd.
Work 5 rnds in twisted rib.
Inc rnd Knit, inc 41 (44, 46) sts evenly around—171 (180, 198) sts.
Change to larger circular needle.
Beg with rnd 1, work in cable pat until piece measures 8 (9½, 10½)"/20.5 (24, 26.5)cm from beg, end 3 (3, 4) sts before

Gauges
18 sts and 34 rnds to 4"/10cm over garter st using larger needles.
27 sts and 30 rnds to 4"/10cm over cable pat using larger needles. *Take time to check gauges.*

beg-of-rnd marker.

Next rnd Work 6 (6, 8) sts in pat then place on st holder for right underarm, work 80 (84, 91) sts in pat for back, work 6 (6, 8) sts in pat then place on st holder for left underarm, work rem 79 (84, 91) sts in pat for front—159 (168, 182) sts.

YOKE

Next rnd With circular needle, work 80 (84, 91) sts in pat (back), pm, p36 (38, 40) sts from first sleeve holder (left sleeve), pm, work rem 79 (84, 91) sts in pat (front), pm, p36 (38, 40) sts from second sleeve holder (right sleeve)—231 (244, 262) sts. Join and pm for beg of rnd. Work 1 rnd across all sts, working cable pat on front and back and garter st on sleeves.

Keeping continuity of cable pat and garter st, work raglan shaping as foll:

Dec rnd 1 *K1, k2tog, pat to 3 sts before next marker, ssk, k1, sm, pat to next marker, sm; rep from * around once more—4 sts dec'd.

Rnd 2 Work even in pat to end of rnd, slipping markers.

Dec rnd 3 *K1, k2tog, pat to 3 sts before next marker, ssk, k1, sm, k2tog, pat to 2 sts before next marker, ssk, sm; rep from * around once more—8 sts dec'd.

Rnd 4 Work even in pat to end of rnd, slipping markers.

Rep these 4 rnds 6 (6, 8) times more—147 (160, 154) sts.

Next rnd Rep dec rnd 3—8 sts dec'd.

Next rnd Work even in pat to end of rnd, slipping markers.

Rep last 2 rnds 3 (4, 2) times more, then rep dec rnd 3 once—107 (112, 122) sts.

NECK SHAPING

Next rnd Work in pat to next marker, sm, work in pat to next marker, sm, work 12 sts in pat, bind off center 17 (20, 23) sts, work 12 sts in pat, sm, work in pat to end. Cut yarn and slip sts after bind-off to LH needle—90 (92, 99) sts.

Cont back and forth in rows on circular needle as foll:

Next row (RS) With RS facing, join yarn to right front neck edge. Bind off 4 sts, work in pat to 3 sts before next marker, ssk, k1, sm, k2tog, work in pat to 2 sts before next marker, ssk, sm, k1, k2tog, work in pat to 3 sts before next marker, ssk, k1, sm, k2tog, work in pat to 2 sts before next marker, ssk, sm, k1, k2tog, pat to end—78 (80, 87) sts.

Next row (WS) Bind off 4 sts, work in pat to end—74 (76, 83) sts.

Next row Bind off 3 sts, ssk, k1, sm, k2tog, work in pat to 2 sts before next marker, ssk, sm, k1, k2tog, work in pat to 3 sts before next marker, ssk, k1, sm, k2tog, work in pat to 2 sts before next marker, ssk, sm, k1, k2tog, pat to end—63 (65, 72) sts.

Next row Bind off 3 sts, work in pat to end—60 (62, 69) sts.

Next row Ssk, k1, sm, [k2tog] 1 (1, 2) times, k4 (4, 2), [ssk] 1 (1, 2) times, sm, k1, [k2tog] 1 (2, 1) times, [k2, k2tog] 8 (8, 9) times, k0 (0, 1), ssk, k1, sm, [k2tog] 1 (1, 2) times, k4 (4, 2), [ssk] 1 (1, 2) times, sm, k1, k2tog—44 (45, 48) sts.

COLLAR

Next row With RS facing and smaller circular needle, pick up and k 30 (37, 40) sts along front neck, k to end of row—74 (82, 88) sts.

Divide sts evenly onto 4 dpn. Join and pm for beg of rnd.

Working in rnds, work in twisted rib until collar measures 4"/10cm.

Bind off loosely in rib.

Finishing

Fold collar in half to WS and whipstitch in place. Sew underarm seams.

Weave in ends and block sweater to measurements. ∎

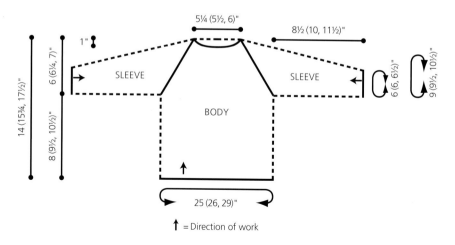

5¼ (5½, 6)"
8½ (10, 11½)"
1"
6 (6¼, 7)"
SLEEVE
SLEEVE
6 (6, 6½)"
9 (9½, 10½)"
14 (15¾, 17½)"
8 (9½, 10½)"
BODY
25 (26, 29)"
↑ = Direction of work

Ruffled Vest

Ruffled puff sleeves cap off this precious vest, fastened at the neck with a single button.

DESIGNED BY AUDREY DRYSDALE

Sizes
Instructions are written for sizes 2 (4, 6). Shown in size 4.

Knitted Measurements
Chest (closed) 23½ (25½, 7½)"/ 60.5 (65, 70)cm
Length 12¼ (13½, 15)"/31 (34.5, 38)cm

Materials
■ 2 3½oz/100g skeins (each approx 213yd/195m) of Cascade Yarns *Pacific* (acrylic/superwash merino wool) in #7 Baby Turquoise (**4**)
■ One pair size 7 (4.5mm) needles, *or size to obtain gauge*
■ One size G/6 (4mm) crochet hook, for edging
■ One ½"/13mm button
■ 2 stitch markers
■ Stitch holders

Note
Body is worked in one piece to the armhole.

Seed St
(over an odd number of sts)
Row 1 (RS) K1, *p1, k1; rep from * to end.

Row 2 K the purl sts and p the knit sts. Rep row 2 for seed st.

Body
Cast on 105 (115, 123) sts. Work in seed st until piece measures 7 (8, 9)"/18 (20.5, 23)cm from beg, end with a WS row.

DIVIDE FOR FRONTS AND BACK
Row 1 (RS) Work 23 (26, 28) sts and slip sts to st holder for right front, bind off next 6 sts, work in pat until there are 47 (51, 55) sts on needle after bind-off and slip sts to st holder for back, bind off next 6 sts, work in pat to end.
Work on 23 (26, 28) left front sts only as foll:

ARMHOLE SHAPING
Next row (WS) Work even in pat.
Dec row (RS) K2tog, work in pat to end.
Rep last 2 rows twice more —20 (23, 25) sts.
Work in pat until armhole measures 2¾ (3, 3½)"/7 (7.5, 9)cm, end with a RS row.

NECK SHAPING
Next row (WS) Bind off 6 (7, 7) sts, work in pat to end—14 (16, 18) sts.
Dec 1 st at neck edge (end of RS rows, beg of WS rows) *every* row 3 times, then at end of every RS row 1 (2, 2) times more —10 (11, 13) sts.
Work in pat until armhole measures 4¾ (5, 5½)"/12 (12.5, 14)cm, end with a WS row.

SHOULDER SHAPING
Bind off 5 (5, 6) sts at beg of next RS

Gauge
18 sts and 28 rows to 4"/10cm over seed st using size 7 (4.5mm) needles.
Take time to check gauge.

row, then bind off rem 5 (6, 7) sts at beg of next RS row.

BACK

Place 47 (51, 55) sts from back holder onto needle, ready for a WS row.
Next row (WS) Work even in pat.
Dec row K2tog, work in pat to last 2 sts, ssk—45 (49, 53) sts.
Rep last 2 rows twice more—41 (45, 49) sts.

Work in pat until armhole measures 4¾ (5, 5½)"/12 (12.5, 14)cm, end with a RS row.

SHOULDER SHAPING

Bind off 5 (5, 6) sts at beg of next 2 rows, then bind off 5 (6, 7) sts at beg of next 2 rows. Bind off rem 21 (23, 23) sts.

RIGHT FRONT

Place 23 (26, 28) sts from right front holder onto needle, ready for a WS row.
Next row (WS) Work in pat to end.
Dec row Work in pat to last 2 sts, ssk.
Rep last 2 rows twice more—20 (23, 25) sts.
Work in pat until armhole measures 2¾ (3, 3½)"/7 (7.5, 9)cm, end with a WS row.

NECK SHAPING

Next row (RS) Bind off 6 (7, 7) sts, work in pat to end—14 (16, 18) sts.
Dec 1 st at neck edge (end of WS rows, beg of RS rows) *every* row 3 times, then at beg of every RS row 1 (2, 2) times more—10 (11, 13) sts.
Work in pat until armhole measures 4¾ (5, 5½)"/12 (12.5, 14)cm, end with a RS row.

SHOULDER SHAPING

Bind off 5 (5, 6) sts at beg of next WS row, then bind off rem 5 (6, 7) sts at beg of next WS row.

Sleeves

Cast on 61 (63, 67) sts.
Work 1 RS row in seed st.

SHAPE CAP

Bind off 3 sts at beg of next 8 rows—37 (39, 43) sts.
Dec row (WS) K2tog, pat to last 2 sts, ssk.
Rep dec row every row 10 (10, 12) times more, end with a WS row—15 (17, 17) sts. Bind off rem sts.

Finishing

Weave in ends and block pieces to measurements. Sew shoulder seams. Place markers on each side of armhole, 4 (4¼, 4¾)"/10 (11, 12)cm down from shoulder seam. Sew a gathering/running st along each bound-off edge of sleeve. Adjust gathering to ease sleeve into armhole between markers. Sew in sleeves.

EDGING

With RS facing and crochet hook, join yarn with sl st at lower corner of right front. Work sc evenly around right front edge, neck edge, and left front edge, working 3 sc into each corner. Fasten off.

BUTTON LOOP

With RS facing and crochet hook, join yarn with sl st in 5th sc down from corner of right front neck edge. Ch 4, skip next 2 sc, sl st in next sc. Fasten off. Sew button to left front opposite loop. ∎

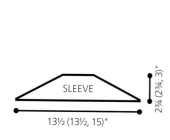

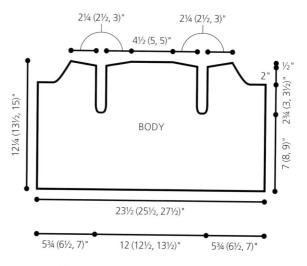

Raccoon Blanket

A trio of button-eyed, fluffy-tailed bandits sit atop leafy branches on this three-dimensional intarsia blanket.

DESIGNED BY AMY BAHRT

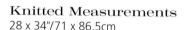

Knitted Measurements
28 x 34"/71 x 86.5cm

Materials
- 3 3½oz/100g skeins (each approx 213yd/195m) of Cascade Yarns *Pacific* (acrylic/superwash merino wool) each in #64 Stonewash Heather (B) and #59 Milk Chocolate (C) (4)
- 2 skeins in #33 Cactus (A)
- 1 skein each in #42 Espresso (D) and #01 Cream (E)
- Size 7 (4.5mm) circular needle, 32"/80cm long, *or size to obtain gauge*
- Two size 7 (4.5mm) double-pointed needles (dpn)
- Size G/6 (4mm) crochet hook
- Three ⅜"/10mm white four-hole buttons
- Stitch markers
- Needle and matching thread
- Small amount of polyester stuffing

Bark Pattern #1
(over 20 sts)
Rows 1–4 Work in St st (k on RS, p on WS).
Rows 5 and 7 K3, [p2, k4] twice, p2, k3.
Rows 6 and 8 P3, [k2, p4] twice, k2, p3.
Rows 9–12 Work in St st.
Rows 13 and 15 [P2, k4] 3 times, p2.
Rows 14 and 16 [K2, p4] 3 times, k2.
Rep rows 1–16 for bark pat #1.

Bark Pattern #2
(over 53 sts)
Rows 1 and 2 Work in St st.
Rows 3 and 5 [K4, p2] 8 times, k5.
Rows 4 and 6 P5, [k2, p4] 8 times.
Rows 7–10 Work in St st.
Rows 11 and 13 K1, [p2, k4] 8 times, p2, k2.
Rows 12 and 14 P2, [k2, p4] 8 times, k2, p1.
Rows 15 and 16 Work in St st.

Bark Pattern #3
(over 53 sts)
Rows 1 and 2 Work in St st.
Rows 3 and 5 K5, [p2, k4] 8 times.
Rows 4 and 6 [P4, k2] 8 times, p5.
Rows 7–10 Work in St st.
Rows 11 and 13 K2, [p2, k4] 8 times, p2, k1.
Rows 12 and 14 P1, [k2, p4] 8 times, k2, p2.
Rows 15 and 16 Work in St st.

Notes
1) Join new balls of yarn for garter borders

Gauge
20 sts and 26 rows to 4"/10cm over St st using size 7 (4.5mm) needles.
Take time to check gauge.

and each large block of color. Do *not* carry yarn behind center trunk or charts.
2) When changing colors, twist yarns on WS to prevent holes in work.
3) Charts are worked in St st.

Blanket

With circular needle and A, cast on 136 sts. Work in garter st (k every row) for 8 rows.

BEGIN BARK PATTERN #1
Row 1 (RS) With A, k5 (garter st border); with B, k53; with C, k20 for first row of bark pattern #1; join 2nd ball of B and k53; join 2nd ball of A and k5 (garter st border).
Row 2 With A, k5; with B, p53; with C, work row 2 of bark pattern #1 over 20 sts; with B, p53; with A, k5.
Cont to work bark pattern #1 in this way through row 16, maintaining garter st borders with A and rem sts with B in St st (k on RS, p on WS) as established, then work rows 1–10 once more.

BEGIN BARK PATTERN #2
Note Cont to work bark pattern #1 as established over center 20 sts until top garter border.
Row 1 (RS) With A, k5; with B, k53; with C, work row 11 of bark pattern #1; with C, work row 1 of bark pattern #2 over 53 sts; with A, k5.
Row 2 With A, k5; with C, work row 2 of bark pattern #2; with C, work row 12 of bark pattern #1; with B, p53; with A, k5.
Cont to work bark patterns #1 and #2 as established until 16 rows of bark pattern #2 are complete.
Next row (RS) With A, k5; with B, k53; with C, work bark pattern #1 as established over 20 sts; with B, k53; with A, k5.
Cont in pats as established until 16 rows

of bark pattern #1 have been worked 3 times total from beg, then work rows 1–10 once more (58 rows of bark pattern #1 have been worked).

BEGIN BARK PATTERN #3
Row 1 (RS) With A, k5; with C, work row 1 of bark pattern #3 over 53 sts; with C, work row 11 of bark pattern #1; with B, k53; with A, k5.
Row 2 With A, k5; with B, p53; with C, work row 12 of bark pattern 1; with C, work row 2 of bark pattern #3 over 53 sts; with A, k5.
Cont to work bark patterns #1 and #3 as established until 16 rows of bark pattern #3 are complete.

BEGIN CHART 1
Row 1 (RS) With A, k5; with B, k13; work chart 1 over 28 sts; with B, k12; with C, work in bark pattern #1 as established over 20 sts; with B, k53; with A, k5.
Cont to work chart in this way through row 24 of chart 1.

BEGIN BARK PATTERN #2
Row 25 With A, k5; with B, k13, work chart 1 over 28 sts; with B, k12; with C, work in bark pattern #1 as established over 20 sts; with C, work row 1 of bark pattern #2 over 53 sts; with A, k5.
Row 26 With A, k5; with C, work row 2 of bark pattern #2 over 53 sts; with C, work bark pattern #1 as established; with B, p12; work chart 1 over 28 sts; with B, p13; with A, k5.
Next row (RS) With A, k5; with B, k53; with C, work bark pattern #1; with C, work row 3 of bark pattern #2 over 53 sts; with A, k5.
Next row With A, k5; with C, work row 4 of bark pattern #2; with C, work bark

pattern #1; with B, p53; with A, k5.
Cont to work bark patterns #1 and #2 as established until 16 rows of bark pattern #2 are complete.

BEGIN CHART 2
Row 1 (RS) With A, k5; with B, k53; with C, work bark pattern #1; with B, k12; work chart 2 over 28 sts; with B, k13; with A, k5.
Cont to work chart in this way through row 16 of chart.

BEGIN BARK PATTERN #3
Row 17 With A, k5; with C, work row 1 of bark pattern #3 over 53 sts; with C, work bark pattern #1; with B, k12; work chart over 28 sts; with B, k13; with A, k5.
Cont to work patterns as established until chart 2 is complete.
Next row (RS) With A, k5; with C, work bark pattern #3 over 53 sts; with C, work bark pattern #1; with B, k53; with A, k5.
Cont to work bark patterns #1 and #3 as established until 16 rows of bark pattern #3 are complete.

BEGIN CHART 1
Row 1 (RS) With A, k5; with B, k13; work chart 1 over 28 sts; with B, k12; with C, work in bark pattern #1 as established over 20 sts; with B, k53; with A, k5.
Cont to work chart in this way through row 24 of chart.

BEGIN BARK PATTERN #2
Row 25 With A, k5; with B, k13; work chart 1 over 28 sts; with B, k12; with C, work in bark pattern #1 as established over 20 sts; with C, work row 1 of bark pattern #2 over 53 sts; with A, k5.
Row 26 With A, k5; with C, work row 2 of bark pattern #2 over 53 sts; with C,

work bark pattern #1 as established; with B, p12; work chart 1 over 28 sts; with B, p13; with A, k5.

Next row (RS) With A, k5; with B, k53; with C, work bark pattern #1; with C, work row 3 of bark pattern #2 over 53 sts; with A, k5.

Next row With A, k5; with C, work row 4 of bark pattern #2; with C, work bark pattern #1; with B, p53; with A, k5.

Cont to work bark patterns #1 and #2 as established until 16 rows of bark pattern #2 are complete.

Next row (RS) With A, k5; with B, k53; with C, work bark pattern #1; with B, k53, with A, k5.

Next row With A, k5; with B, p53; with C, work bark pattern #1; with B, p53; with A, k5.

Rep last 2 rows 7 times more.

With A, work 7 rows in garter st over all sts. Bind off on WS.

Finishing

Block lightly to measurements.

Forming an X with thread, attach buttons for eyes as indicated on charts. With D, work French knot noses as indicated on chart.

EARS (MAKE 3)

With crochet hook and C, ch 10. Allow ch to swirl to form small circle and tack one edge in place as indicated on chart.

TAILS (MAKE 3)

With dpn and D, cast on 5 sts. Work 4 rows in St st.

Working in St st, repeat 4-row stripe pat as foll: 2 rows C, 2 rows D, AT THE SAME TIME, work as foll:

Next (inc) row (RS) Kfb, k to last st, kfb—2 sts inc'd.

Next row Purl.

Rep last 2 rows 4 times more—15 sts.

Work 10 rows even in stripe pat.

Next (dec) row (RS) K2tog, k to last 2 sts, k2tog—2 sts dec'd.

Next row Purl.

Rep last 2 rows 4 times more—5 sts.

Cut yarn, leaving a long end. Pull through rem sts to gather, then use end to sew tail seam, lightly stuffing with fiberfill. Attach end of tail as indicated on chart.

LEAVES (MAKE 3)

With dpn and A, cast on 3 sts.

*Knit one row. Without turning work, slide the sts back to the opposite end of needle to work next row from RS. Pull yarn tightly from the end of the row. Rep from * for I-cord for 3 rows.

Next row (inc) Kfb, k to last st, kfb—2 sts inc'd.

Next row Purl.

Rep last 2 rows twice more—9 sts.

Next row (dec) K2tog, k to last 2 sts, k2tog—2 sts dec'd.

Next row Purl.

Rep last 2 rows twice more—3 sts.

Next row K3tog. Fasten off last st.

Sew leaves to trunk, using photo as guide. ∎

Raccoon Blanket

45

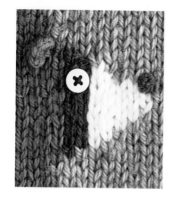

Chart 1

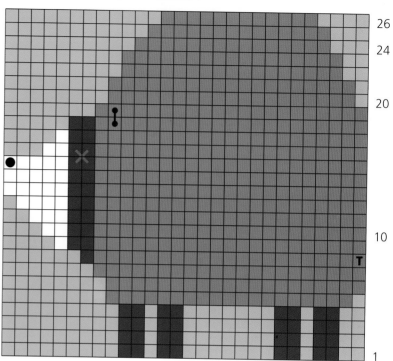

26
24
20
10
T
1

28 sts

Chart 2

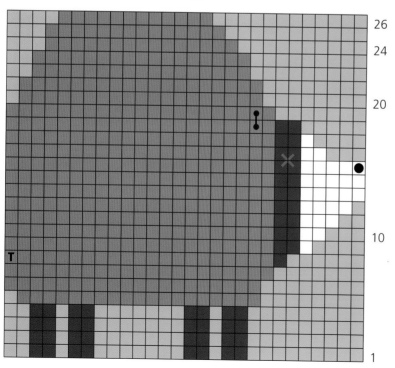

26
24
20
10
T
1

28 sts

Color Key

▨	Stonewash Heather (B)
▨	Milk Chocolate (C)
▨	Espresso (D)
☐	Cream (E)
⊠	eye placement
◉	nose placement
T	tail placement
♀	ear placement

Bright Pockets Cardi

Bright patch pockets update this classic striped raglan and give kids a perfect place to stash treasures and toys.

DESIGNED BY MELISSA McGILL

Sizes
Instructions are written for sizes 2 (4, 6). Shown in size 2.

Knitted Measurements
Chest (closed) 26 (28, 30½)"/64.5 (71, 77.5)cm
Length 15 (16½, 17¾)"/38 (42, 45)cm
Upper arm 10 (10½, 11)"/25.5 (26.5, 28)cm

Materials
■ 2 3½oz/100g skeins (each approx 213yd/195m) of Cascade Yarns *Pacific* (acrylic/superwash merino wool) in #61 Silver (MC) (**4**)
■ 2 skeins #02 White (A)
■ 1 skein #21 Aquamarine (B)
■ One size 7 (4.5mm) circular needle, 24"/60cm long, *or size to obtain gauge*
■ One pair each size 6 and 7 (4 and 4.5mm) needles
■ 5 (5, 6) ⅝"/17mm buttons
■ Stitch markers
■ Stitch holders

Notes
1) Body is worked in one piece to arm-holes.
2) Body and sleeves are worked separately and joined when working the yoke.
3) Circular needles are used on the body

to accommodate the large number of sts. Do *not* join. Work back and forth in rows.

Stripe Pattern
Worked in St st (k on RS, p on WS) as foll:
4 rows A, 4 rows MC.
Rep these 8 rows for stripe pat.

K2, P2 Rib
(over multiple of 4 sts plus 2)
Row 1 (RS) K2, *p2, k2; rep from * to end.
Row 2 P2, *k2, p2; rep from * to end.
Rep rows 1 and 2 for k2, p2 rib.

Sleeves
With larger needles and MC, cast on 34 sts. Work 5 rows in k2, p2 rib, end with a RS row. Purl 1 WS row.
Work in St st and stripe pat, inc 1 st each side of 5th and every foll 4th row 2 (0, 0) times, then every 6th row 5 (8, 9) times—50 (52, 56) sts.
Work even in pat until piece measures approx 8½ (9½, 10¼)"/21.5 (24, 26)cm from beg, end with a RS row.
Next row (WS) Bind off 3 sts, work in pat to last 3 sts, bind off 3 sts—44 (46, 50) sts. Place rem sts on holder and set aside.

Body
With circular needle and MC, cast on 142 (154, 170) sts.
Work 5 rows in k2, p2 rib, end with a RS row.
Dec row (WS) Purl, dec 18 (18, 22) sts evenly across—124 (136, 148) sts.
Work in St st and stripe pat until piece measures approx 8½ (9½,10¼)"/21.5 (24, 26)cm from beg, end with same row of stripe pat as for the sleeves and a RS row.
Next row (WS) Work 27 (30, 33) sts in pat for left front, bind off next 6 sts, cont in pat until there are 58 (64, 70) sts on needle after bind-off for back, bind off next 6 sts, work rem 27 (30, 33) sts in pat for right front—112 (124, 136) sts.

Gauge
20 sts and 26 rows to 4"/10cm over St st using larger needles. *Take time to check gauge.*

Yoke

Cont in St st and stripe pat as foll:

Row 1 (RS) K27 (30, 33) for right front, pm, k44 (46, 50) from first sleeve, pm, k58 (64, 70) for back, pm, k44 (46, 50) from second sleeve, pm, k27 (30, 33) for left front—200 (216, 236) sts.

Row 2 Purl.

Dec row *K to 3 sts before next marker, ssk, k1, sm, k1, k2tog; rep from * 3 times more, k to end—192 (208, 228) sts.

Next row Purl.

Rep last 2 rows 14 (15, 17) times more—80 (88, 92) sts.

NECK SHAPING

Row 1 (RS) Bind off 3 (4, 4) sts, *k to 3 sts before next marker, ssk, k1, sm, k1, k2tog; rep from * 3 times more, k to end—69 (76, 80) sts.

Row 2 Bind off 3 (4, 4) sts, p to end—66 (72, 76) sts.

Row 3 Bind off 2 (3, 3) sts, *k to 3 sts before next marker, ssk, k1, sm, k1, k2tog; rep from * 3 times more, k to end—56 (61, 65) sts.

Row 4 Bind off 2 (3, 3) sts, p to end—54 (58, 62) sts.

Bind off rem 54 (58, 62) sts.

Finishing

Block to measurements.
Sew underarm seams.

NECKBAND

With RS facing, smaller needles, and MC, pick up and k 62 (66, 70) sts evenly around neck opening. Beg with row 2, work k2, p2 rib for 5 rows, end with a WS row. Bind off loosely in rib.

BUTTON BAND

With RS facing, smaller needles, and MC, pick up and k 74 (82, 90) sts evenly along right front edge (for boys) or left front edge (for girls). Beg with row 2, work in k2, p2 rib for 9 rows, end with a WS row. Bind off loosely in rib.

BUTTONHOLE BAND

With RS facing, smaller needles, and MC, pick up and k 74 (82, 90) sts evenly along left front edge (for boys) or right front edge (for girls). Beg with row 2, work in k2, p2 rib for 4 rows, end with a RS row.

Buttonhole row (WS) Rib first 4 sts, *bind off next 2 sts, rib until 14 (16, 14) sts on RH needle; rep from * 3 (3, 4) times more, bind off next 2 sts, rib to end.

Next row (RS) Rib to end, casting on 2 sts over each set of bound-off sts.
Work 3 rows more in rib. Bind off loosely in rib.
Sew buttons opposite buttonholes.

POCKETS

With larger needles and B, cast on 18 sts. Beg with a knit (RS) row, work 14 (16, 16) rows in St st, end with a WS row. Work 4 rows in k2, p2 rib, end with a WS row. Bind off loosely in rib. Sew pockets to fronts, with cast-on edge approx 2¼"/3cm up from lower edge and 1"/2.5cm in from center front edge. ■

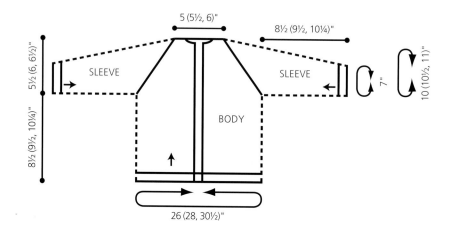

5 (5½, 6)"

8½ (9½, 10¼)"

5½ (6, 6½)"

SLEEVE

SLEEVE

8½ (9½, 10¼)"

7"

10 (10½, 11)"

BODY

26 (28, 30½)"

47

Cabled Hat

This plush cabled hat is worked seamlessly in the round.
Make it extra-special with three decorative buttons.

DESIGNED BY KIRI FITZGERALD-HILLIER

Knitted Measurements
Brim circumference 16"/40.5cm
Length 7"/18cm

Materials
■ 1 3½oz/100g skein (each approx
213yd/195m) of Cascade Yarns *Pacific*
(acrylic/superwash merino wool)
in #37 Clover (**4**)
■ One set (5) size 8 (5mm) double-pointed
needles (dpn), *or size to obtain gauge*
■ Stitch markers
■ Cable needle (cn)
■ Three 1⅛"/29mm decorative buttons

Stitch Glossary
4-st RC Sl 2 sts to cn and hold to *back*,
k2, k2 from cn.
4-st LC Sl 2 sts to cn and hold to *front*,
k2, k2 from cn.
4-st RPC Sl 2 sts to cn and hold to *back*,
k2, p2 from cn.
4-st LPC Sl 2 sts to cn and hold to *front*,
p2, k2 from cn.

Cable Pattern 1
(over a multiple of 12 sts)
Rnds 1–3 Knit.
Rnd 4 *4-st RC, k4, 4-st LC; rep from * around.

Rnds 5–7 Knit.
Rnd 8 *K2, 4-st LC, 4-st RC, k2; rep from *
around.
Rep rnds 1–8 for cable pat 1.

Cable Pattern 2
(over a multiple of 12 sts)
Rnds 1–3 Knit.
Rnd 4 *4-st RC, k4, 4-st LC; rep from * around.
Rnd 5 *P1, k10, p1; rep from * around.
Rnds 6 and 7 *P2, k8, p2; rep from * around.
Rnd 8 *P2, 4-st LPC, 4-st RPC, p2; rep
from * around.
Rep rnds 1–8 for cable pat 2.

Hat
Cast on 96 sts, divided evenly over 4 dpn.
Join, taking care not to twist sts, and pm
for beg of rnd.
Work rnds 1–8 of cable pat 1 four times.
Work rnds 1–8 of cable pat 2 once.

CROWN SHAPING
Rnd 1 *P4, k4, p4; rep from * around.
Dec rnd 2 *P2, p2tog tbl, k4, p2tog, p2;
rep from * around—80 sts.
Rnds 3 and 4 *P3, k4, p3; rep from * around.
Dec rnd 5 *P1, p2tog tbl, k4, p2tog, p1;
rep from * around—64 sts.
Rnd 6 *P2, k4, p2; rep from * around.
Dec rnd 7 *P2tog tbl, k4, p2tog; rep
from * around—48 sts.
Dec rnd 8 *K2tog, k2, ssk; rep from *
around—32 sts.
Dec rnd 9 *K2tog, ssk; rep from *
around—16 sts.
Dec rnd 10 *K2tog; rep from *
around—8 sts.
Cut yarn and pull through rem sts, draw
up and secure.

Finishing
Weave in ends. Sew buttons to hat, using
photo as guide. ■

Gauge
24 sts and 30 rnds to 4"/10cm over cable pat 1 using size 8 (5mm) needles. *Take time to check gauge.*

48

Zip-Front Jacket

Worked in a checkered slip-stitch pattern, this moto jacket is perfect for tricycling around the neighborhood.

DESIGNED BY KATHARINE HUNT

Sizes
Instructions are written for sizes 2 (4, 6). Shown in size 6.

Knitted Measurements
Chest (closed) 24½ (26¾, 29)"/62 (68, 73.5)cm
Length 14½ (16, 16½)"/37 (40.5, 42)cm
Upper arm 12 (13½, 14½)"/30.5 (34, 37)cm

Materials
■ 2 (3, 3) 3½oz/100g skeins (each approx 213yd/195m) of Cascade Yarns *Pacific* (acrylic/superwash merino wool) in #94 Black (A) (4)
■ 2 skeins in #61 Grey (B)
■ 1 skein in #43 Red (C)
■ One each sizes 5 and 6 (3.75 and 4mm) circular needle, 29"/74cm long, *or size to obtain gauges*
■ One pair each sizes 5 and 6 (3.75 and 4mm) needles
■ One size E/4 (3.5mm) crochet hook
■ Stitch holders or waste yarn
■ One 12 (12, 14)"/30 (30, 35)cm separating zipper
■ Matching sewing thread

Note
Circular needles are used to accommodate large number of stitches. Do *not* join.

Blister Pattern Stitch
(over a multiple of 6 sts plus 4)
Row 1 (RS) With A, knit.
Row 2 (WS) With A, purl.
Row 3 With B, k1, *sl 2 wyib, k4; rep from *, end sl 2 wyib, k1.
Row 4 With B, p1, *sl 2 wyif, p4; rep from *, end sl 2 wyif, p1.
Rows 5 and 6 Rep rows 3 and 4.
Row 7 With A, knit.
Row 8 With A, purl.
Row 9 With B, k4, *sl 2 wyib, k4; rep from * to end.
Row 10 With B, p4, *sl 2 wyif, p4; rep from * to end.
Rows 11 and 12 Rep rows 9 and 10.
Rep rows 1–12 for blister pat st.

Stripe Pattern
With B, knit 1 row, purl 1 row; with C, knit 1 row, purl 1 row; with B, knit 1 row, purl 1 row.

K1, P1 Rib
(over an odd number of sts)
Row 1 (RS) K1, *p1, k1; rep from * to end.
Row 2 P1, *k1, p1; rep from * to end.
Rep rows 1 and 2 for k1, p1 rib.

Body
With smaller circular needle and A, cast on 135 (147, 159) sts. Working back and forth, work in k1, p1 rib for 7 rows.
Inc row (WS) Work in rib, inc 7 sts

Gauges
21 sts and 29 rows to 4"/10cm over St st using larger needles.
23 sts and 34 rows to 4"/10cm over blister pat st using larger needles. *Take time to check gauges.*

evenly spaced across—142 (154, 166) sts. Work stripe pattern once. Change to larger circular needle.

BEGIN BLISTER PATTERN

Work in blister pat st until piece measures 9 (9½, 9½)"/23 (24, 24)cm from beg, end with pat row 6 or 12.

DIVIDE FOR FRONT AND BACK

Next row (RS) With A, k33 (36, 39) sts for right front and place sts on holder, bind off 6 sts, k until there are 64 (70, 76) sts on needle for back, place rem 39 (42, 45) sts on holder.

Back

Cont in blister pattern, work as foll:
Next row (WS) Work even in pat.
Dec row (RS) K1, ssk, work to last 3 sts, k2tog, k1—2 sts dec'd.
Rep dec row every other row 17 (18, 21) times, then every 4th row 2 (3, 3) times—24 (26, 26) sts.
Work 1 row even. Bind off.

Left Front

Transfer sts from left front holder to needle ready to work a RS row.
Next row (RS) Bind off 6 sts, work to end—33 (36, 39) sts.
Next row (WS) Purl.
Dec row K1, ssk, work to end—1 st dec'd.
Rep dec row every other row 12 (14, 18) times more—20 (21, 20) sts.
Work 1 RS row even.

NECK SHAPING

Next row (WS) Bind off 3 (4, 4) sts, work to end. Cont to shape neck, dec 1 st at neck edge (end of RS rows, beg of WS rows) every row 4 times, then every RS row 4 times. AT THE SAME TIME, cont

to shape raglan armhole by dec every other row 5 (4, 3) times more, then every 4th row 2 (3, 3) times—2 sts.
Work 1 row even. Bind off.

Right Front

Transfer sts from right front holder to needle to work next row from WS. Work armhole shaping as foll:
Next row (WS) Work even in pat.
Dec row Work to last 3 sts, k2tog, k1—1 st dec'd.
Rep dec row every other row 12 (14, 18) times more—20 (21, 20) sts, end with a WS row.

NECK SHAPING

Next row (RS) Bind off 3 (4, 4) sts, work to end. Cont to shape neck, dec 1 st at

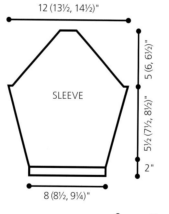

neck edge (beg of RS rows, end of WS rows) every row 4 times, then every RS row 4 times. AT THE SAME TIME, cont to shape raglan armhole by dec every other row 5 (4, 3) times more, then every 4th row 2 (3, 3) times—2 sts.
Work 1 row even. Bind off.

Sleeves

With smaller needles and A, cast on 31 (33, 37) sts. Work in k1, p1 rib for 8 rows, inc 12 sts evenly spaced across last WS row—43 (45, 49) sts.
Work stripe pat once.
Change to larger needles and cont with A only to end of sleeve as foll:
Work in St st (k on RS, p on WS) for 3 rows.
Inc row (RS) K1, kfb, k to the last 3 sts, kfb, k2.
Rep inc row every 4th row 9 (12, 13) times more—63 (71, 77) sts.
Work even until piece measures 7½ (9½, 10½)"/19 (24, 26.5)cm from beg, end with a WS row.

RAGLAN CAP SHAPING

Bind off 3 sts at beg of next 2 rows—57 (65, 71) sts.
Dec row 1 (RS) K1, ssk, k to last 3 sts, k2tog, k1—2 sts dec'd.

12 (13½, 14½)"

SLEEVE

5 (6, 6½)"

5½ (7½, 8½)"

2"

8 (8½, 9¼)"

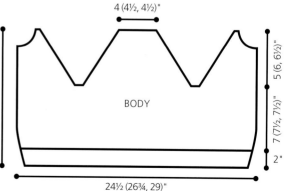

4 (4½, 4½)"

14 (15½, 16)"

BODY

5 (6, 6½)"

7 (7½, 7½)"

2"

24½ (26¾, 29)"

Dec row 2 (WS) P1, p2tog, p to last 3 sts, p2tog tbl, p1—2 sts dec'd.
Rep dec rows 1 and 2 one (two, two) times more.
Next row (RS) Rep dec row 1.
Next row (WS) Purl.
Rep the last 2 rows 18 (20, 23) times more—11 sts. Bind off.

Finishing
Block pieces to measurements.
Sew raglan sleeves into armholes.
Sew sleeve seams.

NECKBAND
With smaller needles and A, pick up and k 25 (26, 26) sts from shaped right neck edge, 9 sts from top of sleeve, 25 (27, 27) sts across back neck, 9 sts from top of sleeve, 25 (26, 26) sts from shaped left neck edge—93 (97, 97) sts.
Beg with WS row 2 of rib, work in k1, p1 rib for 2"/5cm. Bind off loosely in rib.

FRONT EDGE TRIM
Row 1 (RS) With crochet hook and A, work an edge of sl st along center front edge, turn.
Row 2 (WS) Ch 1, work an edge of sl st to the inside of the sl st row worked before, turn.
Row 3 Ch 1, work 1 sl st in outside loop of each sl st of the first row. Fasten off.

ZIPPER
Pin, then baste, the zipper in place along the center front. Sew zipper in place with thread, using one row of backstitch next to the zipper teeth and one row of whip-stitch along the outer edge of the zipper tape to hold in place. ∎

Ribbed Hat

This sleek, stretchy hat is a cinch to knit,
and it fits little heads like a dream.

DESIGNED BY KIRI FITZGERALD-HILLIER

Knitted Measurements
Brim Circumference (unstretched)
14"/35.5cm (hat will stretch to fit most)
Length (with brim folded) 7½"/19cm

Materials
■ 1 3½oz/100g skein (each approx
120yd/110m) of Cascade Yarns *Pacific
Chunky* (acrylic/superwash merino wool)
in #40 Peacock or #95 Lime Green (5)
■ One set (5) size 10 (6mm)
double-pointed needles (dpn),
or size to obtain gauge
■ One size J/10 (6mm) crochet hook
■ Stitch marker

Chain Cast-On
Make a slipknot and place on crochet
hook. Holding the hook in your right
hand and needle in your left, loop
working yarn over left index finger.
*Bring the hook over the top of needle
and under the strand on finger, catch
yarn, and pull yarn over needle and
through loop on crochet hook. Bring
working yarn to the back of needle.
Rep from * until there is one less stitch
than required. Slip the remaining loop
from the hook to the needle.

Hat
Cast on 55 sts using chain cast-on.
Divide sts evenly over 4 dpn. Join and pm
for beg of rnd.
Rnd 1 [P4, k1] 11 times.
Rep rnd 1 for p4, k1 rib until piece
measures 9"/23cm from beg.

CROWN SHAPING
Dec rnd 1 [P1, p2tog, p1, k1] 11
times—44 sts.
Rnds 2 and 3 [P3, k1] 11 times.
Dec rnd 4 [P2tog, p1, k1] 11 times—33 sts.
Rnd 5 [P2, k1] 11 times.
Dec rnd 6 [P2tog, k1] 11 times—22 sts.
Dec rnd 7 [K2tog] 11 times—11 sts.
Cut yarn and pull through rem sts, draw
up and secure.

Finishing
Weave in ends. Fold brim approx
3"/7.5cm to RS. ■

Gauge
16 sts and 20 rnds to 4"/10cm over p4, k1 rib using size 10 (6mm) needles.
Take time to check gauge.

Checkered Dress

Perfect for any occasion, this special frock is finished with dressmaker details like I-cord piping, a zipper closure, and a collar stand.

DESIGNED BY LINDA MEDINA

Sizes
Instructions are written for sizes 2 (4, 6). Shown in size 6.

Knitted Measurements
Chest 21 (22¾, 24½)"/53.5 (58, 62)cm
Length 16 (18, 20½)"/40.5 (45.5, 52)cm

Materials
- 2 3½oz/100g skeins (each approx 213yd/195m) of Cascade Yarns *Pacific* (acrylic/superwash merino wool) each in #45 Concord Grape (A), #43 Ruby (B), and #09 Sand (C) (5)
- One size 7 (4.5mm) circular needle, 32"/80cm long, *or size to obtain gauges*
- One pair size 7 (4.5mm) straight needles
- One size 6 (4mm) circular needle, 16"/40cm long
- One set (5) size 6 (4mm) double-pointed needles (dpn)
- Stitch markers
- Three ½"/12mm buttons
- One 12"/30cm closed-end zipper
- Matching thread

Notes
1) The skirt is worked back and forth in rows in tweed pat st with the seam up the center back and with the zipper

inserted at the top edge to close.
2) Tweed pat st is worked using one color for each row, changing colors every two rows. Carry colors not in use up the sides of the rows without cutting yarn between the changes.

Tweed Pattern Stitch
(over a multiple of 4 sts plus 3)
Row 1 (RS) With A, k1, *sl 1 wyib, k3;

rep from *, end sl 1 wyib, k1.
Row 2 With A, k1, *sl 1 wyif, take yarn to back and k3; rep from *, end sl 1 wyif, take yarn to back and k1.
Row 3 With B, k3, *sl 1 wyib, k3; rep from * to end.
Row 4 With B, k3, *sl 1 wyif, take yarn to back, k3; rep from * to end.
Rows 5 and 6 With C, rep rows 1 and 2.
Rows 7 and 8 With A, rep rows 3 and 4.
Rows 9 and 10 With B, rep rows 1 and 2.
Rows 11 and 12 With C, rep rows 3 and 4.
Rep rows 1–12 for tweed pat st.

Skirt
With larger circular needle and A, cast on 207 (223, 239) sts.
Work in tweed pat st until piece measures 9 (10½, 12½)"/23 (26.5, 32)cm from beg, end with a RS row.
Dec row (WS) With C, k1, *k2tog; rep from * to end—104 (112, 120) sts.
Note The line that shows on the RS at this row will be the indicated row for the I-cord attachment in the finishing stage.

Bodice
Cut A and B and cont bodice with C only.
Set-up row (RS) With C, k24 (26, 28),

Gauges
19 sts and 26 rows to 4"/10cm over St st, after blocking, using larger needles.
22 sts and 41 rows to 4"/10cm over tweed pat st, after blocking, using larger needles. *Take time to check gauges.*

k2tog, k20 (22, 24), k2tog, k4, pm, k4, k2tog, k20 (22, 24), k2tog, k24 (26, 28)—100 (108, 116) sts.
Row 1 (WS) K1, p to last st, k1.
Row 2 Knit.
Rep rows 1 and 2 for 14 rows more.

DIVIDE FOR FRONT AND BACK
Next row (WS) K1, p20 (22, 24), bind off 8 sts for underarm, p until there are 42 (46, 50) sts from bind-off, bind off 8 sts for underarm, p to last st, k1—21 (23, 25) right back sts; 42 (46, 50) front sts; 21 (23, 25) left back sts. Work the 3 sections separately as foll:

Left Back
Row 1 (RS) Knit.
Row 2 P2tog, p to last st, k1—1 st dec'd.
Rep rows 1 and 2 for 2 (2, 3) times more—18 (20, 21) sts.
Work even, with a k1 st at end of every WS row, until armhole measures 3½, (4, 4½)"/9 (10, 11.5)cm.

NECK SHAPING
Next row (RS) Bind off 9 (9, 10) sts, work to end.
Next row (WS) P to last 2 sts, p2tog—8 (10, 10) sts.

SHOULDER SHAPING
Knit 1 row.
Bind off 3 (4, 4) sts at beg of next 2 WS rows. Bind off rem 2 sts.

Right Back
Rejoin yarn to the 21 (23, 25) right back sts at the armhole edge ready to work a RS row.
Row 1 (RS) Knit.
Row 2 (WS) K1, p to last 2 sts, p2tog.
Rep rows 1 and 2 for 2 (2, 3) times more—18 (20, 21) sts.
Work even, with a k1 st at beg of every

WS row, until armhole measures 3½ (4, 4½)"/9 (10, 11.5)cm, end with a RS row.

NECK SHAPING
Next row (WS) Bind off 9 (9, 10) sts, work to end.
Next row (RS) K to last 2 sts, k2tog—8 (10, 10) sts.

SHOULDER SHAPING
Purl 1 row.
Bind off 3 (4, 4) sts from beg of next 2 RS rows. Bind off rem 2 sts.

Front
Rejoin yarn to the 42 (46, 50) front sts ready work a RS row.
Row 1 (RS) Knit.
Row 2 (WS) P2tog, p to the last 2 sts, p2tog—2 sts dec'd.
Rep rows 1 and 2 for 2 (2, 3) times more—36 (40, 42) sts.
Work even until armhole measures 2 (2½, 3)"/5 (6.5, 7.5)cm.

NECK SHAPING
Next row (RS) K13 (15, 15), join a 2nd ball of yarn and bind off center 10 (10, 12) sts, k to end.
Cont to shape neck, dec 1 st each side of neck *every* row twice, then every RS row 3 times more, AT THE SAME TIME, when armhole measures 4 (4½, 5)"/10 (11.5, 12.5)cm, shape shoulders as foll:

SHOULDER SHAPING
Bind off 3 (4, 4) sts from each shoulder edge twice, then 2 sts once.

Finishing
Sew shoulder seams.

ARMHOLE TRIM
With smaller circular needle and C, pick up and k 58 (63, 68) sts evenly around

armhole edge. Join to work in rnds and pm to mark beg of rnd. Knit 4 rnds. Bind off.

I-CORD TRIM
With dpn and B, cast on 4 sts.
*Row 1 (RS) Knit. Slide sts back to beg of needle to work next row from the RS. Bring yarn around from back. Rep from * until I-cord fits along the bodice edge at top of skirt. Leave sts on hold, then sew the I-cord to the skirt top, adjusting length if necessary before binding off.

ZIPPER
Pin then baste zipper along top 12"/30cm of the back opening. Sew zipper in place with thread, using one row of backstitch next to the zipper teeth and one row of whipstitch along the outer edge of the zipper tape to hold in place. With yarn, sew back seam for the remaining portion of the open back below the zipper.

COLLAR (MAKE 2)
With smaller circular needles and C, cast on 31 (31, 33) sts.
Row 1 (RS) Knit.
Row 2 Pfb (p in front and back of st), p to last st, pfb.
Row 3 K1, M1, k to last st, M1, k1.
Row 4 Purl.
Rows 5–10 Rep rows 3 and 4 for 3 times more—41 (41, 43) sts.
[Knit 1 row, purl 1 row] twice. Bind off. Work 3-st I-cord trim for each collar piece, sew to collar, and finish as for previous I-cord.

BOTTOM BAND
With larger circular needle and A, pick up and k 204 (220, 236) sts evenly along lower edge of skirt. Join to work in rnds and pm to mark beg of rnd. [Purl 1 rnd,

knit 1 rnd] twice. Bind off purlwise.
Block pieces to measurements.

COLLAR STAND

With smaller circular needle and C, from
the RS, pick up and k 85 (85, 89) sts
evenly around neck edge.

Row 1 (WS) Knit (for turning row).
Row 2 (RS) Knit.
Row 3 Purl.

Bind off. Fold collar stand to the WS along
the turning row and whip st in place,
covering the tape of the zipper at the back
neck. Sew the 2 collar pieces to the top of
the collar stand. Join the I-cord with a few
invisible sts at the center front neck. Fold
collar down and steam block in place.
Sew on buttons as in photo. ■

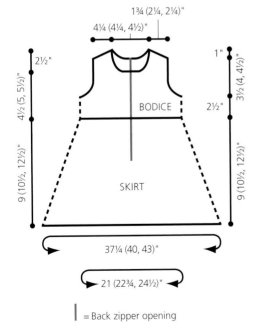

= Back zipper opening

Seed Stitch Cowl

This textured cowl is perfect for keeping kids warm
without slowing them down.

DESIGNED BY AUDREY DRYSDALE

Knitted Measurements
Circumference 22"/56cm
Width 6"/15cm

Materials
■ 1 3½oz/100g skein (each approx
120yd/110m) of Cascade Yarns *Pacific
Chunky* (acrylic/superwash merino wool)
in #106 Carmine Rose (5)
■ One pair size 10 (6mm) needles,
or size to obtain gauge
■ Tapestry needle

Seed Stitch
(over an odd number of sts)
Row 1 (RS) K1, *p1, k1; rep from * to end.
Row 2 K the purl sts and p the knit sts.
Rep row 2 for seed st.

Cowl
Cast on 21 sts. Work in seed st until piece
measures 22"/56cm, ending with a WS row.
Bind off in pat.

Finishing
Twist one end 180 degrees,
sew bound-off and cast-on edges
together. Weave in ends. ■

Gauge
14 sts and 24 rows to 4"/10cm over seed st using size 10 (6mm) needles.
Take time to check gauge.

Seed Stitch Set

Little ones can toddle out in warmth *and* style
in this set of winter accessories.

DESIGNED BY AUDREY DRYSDALE

Knitted Measurements
HAT
Brim circumference 16"/40.5cm
Length to folded brim 7½"/19cm

MITTENS
Hand circumference 7"/18cm
Length 6½"/16.5cm

Materials
HAT
■ 2 3½oz/100g skeins (each approx
120yd/110m) of Cascade Yarns Pacific
Chunky in #106 Carmine Rose (6)
■ One pair size 10 (6mm) needles,
or size to obtain gauges
■ Two size 8 (5mm) double-pointed
needles (dpn)
■ Stitch markers

MITTENS
■ 1 skein in #106 Carmine Rose
■ One pair size 8 (5mm) needles,
or size to obtain gauges
■ Stitch markers

Seed Stitch
(over an odd number of sts)
Row 1 (RS) K1, *p1, k1; rep from * to end.
Row 2 K the purl sts and p the knit sts.
Rep row 2 for seed st.

HAT
With size 10 (6mm) needles, cast on 65 sts.
Row 1 (RS) P1, *k1, p1; rep from * to end.
Row 2 K1, *p1, k1; rep from * to end.
Rep last 2 rows for k1, p1 rib for 4"/10cm,
end with RS row.
Dec row (WS) [Work 6 sts in rib, k2tog]
8 times, k1—57 sts.
Work in seed st over 57 sts until piece measures
7"/18cm from beg, end with a WS row.

CROWN SHAPING
Dec row (RS) K1, p1, k1, *p3tog, [k1, p1]
twice, k1; rep from * to last 6 sts, p3tog,
k1, p1, k1—43 sts.
Work 7 rows even in pat.
Dec row (RS) K1, p1, k1, [p3tog, k1, p1,
k1] 6 times, p3tog, k1—29 sts.
Work 5 rows even in pat.
Dec row (RS) [K1, p3tog] 7 times, k1—15 sts.
Work 1 row even in pat.

Dec row [K2tog] 7 times, k1—8 sts.
Cut yarn and pull through rem sts, draw
up and secure.

EARFLAPS
Place markers along last row of k1, p1 rib
as foll:
Place first set of markers 1½"/4cm from
each edge, place second set of markers
4"/10cm from first marker on each side.
With size 10 (6mm) needles and WS
facing, pick up and k 15 sts between first
and second marker on one side.
Row 1 (WS) Sl 1, p1, [k1, p1] 5 times, k1, p2.
Row 2 Sl 1, k1, [k1, p1] 5 times, k3.
Rep last 2 rows until earflap measures
3"/7.5cm, end with a WS row.

Shape Point
Dec row 1 (RS) Sl 1, k1, p2tog, [k1, p1]
3 times, k1, p2tog, k2—13 sts.
Row 2 Sl 1, p1, [p1, k1] 4 times, p3.
Dec row 3 Sl 1, k1, p2tog, [k1, k1]
twice, p1, p2tog, k2—11 sts.
Row 4 Sl 1, p1, [k1, p1] 3 times, k1, p2.
Dec row 5 Sl 1, k1, p2tog, k1, p1, k1,
p2tog, k2—9 sts.

Gauges
14 sts and 24 rows to 4"/10cm over seed st using size 10 (6mm) needles.
15 sts and 26 rows to 4"/10cm over seed st using size 8 (5mm) needles. *Take time to check gauges*

Row 6 Sl 1, p2, k1, p1, k1, p3.
Dec row 7 Sl 1, k1, p2tog, p1, p2tog, k2—7 sts.
Row 8 Sl 1, [p1, k1] twice, p2.
Row 9 Sl 1, k1, p3tog, k2—5 sts.
Row 10 Sl 1, p1, k1, p2.
Row 11 Sl 1, k1, k2tog, k1—4 sts.

Sl sts to a dpn. With 2nd dpn, *bring yarn behind work and pull firm, k4; rep from * for I-cord until cord measures 10"/25.5cm. Cut yarn and pull through rem sts, draw up and secure end inside cord.
Repeat for 2nd earflap.

Finishing
Sew center back seam. Make a 4"/10cm pompom and secure to top of hat. Fold ribbed brim in half to RS. Weave in ends.

MITTENS
Left Mitten
With size 8 (5mm) needles, cast on 29 sts.
Row 1 (RS) K1, *p1, k1; rep from * to end.
Row 2 P1, *k1, p1; rep from * to end.
Rep last 2 rows for k1, p1 rib for 2"/5cm, end with WS row and dec 2 sts evenly across last row—27 sts.
Work in seed st for 2 rows.

SHAPE THUMB GUSSET
Row 1 (RS) Work 11 sts in pat, pm, [k1, p1, k1] in next st, pm, work 15 sts in pat—29 sts.
Row 2 and all WS rows Work in pat to marker, sm, p to 2nd marker, sm, work in pat to end.
Inc row 3 Work in pat to marker, sm, [kfb] twice, k1, sm, work in pat to end—31 sts.
Row 5 Work in pat to marker, sm, k5, sm, work in pat to end.

Inc row 7 Work in pat to marker, sm, kfb, k2, kfb, k1, sm, work in pat to end—33 sts.
Inc row 9 Work in pat to marker, sm, kfb, k4, kfb, k1, sm, work in pat to end—35 sts.
Row 11 Work in pat to marker, remove marker, k9, remove marker, turn, leaving rem sts unworked.
Working back and forth across 9 thumb sts, work as foll:
Thumb row 1 Cast on 1 st, p10, turn.
Thumb row 2 Cast on 1 st, k11, turn.
Work 5 rows in St st (k on RS, p on WS) over 11 thumb sts.
Next row (RS) [K2tog] 5 times, k1—6 sts.
Cut yarn and pull through rem sts, draw up and secure. Use tail to sew thumb seam.

With RS facing, join yarn at base of thumb ready to work rem 15 sts of row 11. Pick up and k 2 sts at base of thumb, work to end of row in pat.
Next row (WS) Work 15 sts in pat, work 2 picked up sts tog in pat, work to end in pat—27 sts.
Cont in seed st until mitten measures 6"/15cm from beg, end with a WS row.

SHAPE TOP
Dec row 1 (RS) K1, [p3tog, k1] 6 times, p1, k1—15 sts.
Row 2 Work even in pat.
Dec row 3 K1, [p3tog, k1] 3 times, p1, k1—9 sts.
Row 4 Work even in pat.
Dec row 5 [K2tog] 4 times, k1—5 sts.
Cut yarn and pull through rem sts, draw up and secure. Use tail to sew side seam.

Right Mitten
Work as for left mitten to shape thumb gusset.

SHAPE THUMB GUSSET
Row 1 (RS) Work 15 sts in pat, pm, (k1, p1, k1) in next st, pm, work 11 sts in pat—29 sts.
Work to end of shape thumb gusset same as for left mitten.
With RS facing, join yarn at base of thumb ready to work rem 11 sts of row 11. Pick up and k 2 sts at base of thumb, work to end of row in pat.
Next row (WS) Work 11 sts in pat, work 2 picked up sts tog in pat, work to end in pat—27 sts.
Complete same as for left mitten.

Finishing
Weave in ends. ■

53

Lace Pullover

Vines climb up this pullover in a simple lace pattern, while contrast edging gives it a pretty pop.

DESIGNED BY SARA KAY HARTMANN

Sizes
Instructions are written for sizes 2 (4, 6). Shown in size 2.

Knitted Measurement
Chest 24 (27, 30)"/61 (68.5, 76)cm
Length 11 (13½, 15½)"/28 (34, 39.5)cm
Upper arm 9¼ (10, 11)"/23.5 (25.5, 28)cm

Materials
■ 2 (2, 3) 3½oz/100g skeins (each approx 213yd/195m) of Cascade Yarns *Pacific* (acrylic/superwash merino wool) in #15 Taupe (A) ④
■ 1 skein in #95 Lime Green (B)
■ One pair each sizes 6 and 7 (4 and 4.5mm) needles, *or size to obtain gauge*
■ One size 6 (4mm) circular needle, 16"/40cm long
■ One size G/6 (4mm) crochet hook
■ Stitch markers
■ Stitch holders

Note
Lace pattern can be worked by following written instructions or chart.

Lace Pattern
(over a multiple of 8 sts plus 4)
Row 1 (RS) P3, *yo, k2, ssk, k2, p2; rep from * to last st, p1.
Row 2 and all WS rows K the knit sts and p the purl sts and yos.
Row 3 P3, *k1, yo, k2, ssk, k1, p2; rep from * to last st, p1.

Row 5 P3, *k2, yo, k2, ssk, p2; rep from * to last st, p1.
Row 7 P3, *k6, p2; rep from * to last st, p1.
Row 9 P3, *k2, k2tog, k2, yo, p2; rep from * to last st, p1.
Row 11 P3, *k1, k2tog, k2, yo, k1, p2; rep from * to last st, p1.
Row 13 P3, *k2tog, k2, yo, k2, p2; rep from * to last st, p1.
Row 15 P3, *k6, p2; rep from * to last st, p1.
Row 16 K the knit sts and p the purl sts and yos.
Rep rows 1–16 for lace pat.

Back
With smaller needles and A, cast on 60 (68, 76) sts.
Row 1 (WS) K3, *p6, k2; rep from * to last st, k1.
Row 2 P3, *k6, p2; rep from * to last st, p1.
Rep rows 1 and 2 five times more, then rep row 1 once more.

BEGIN LACE PATTERN
Beg with row 1 (RS), work in lace pat until piece measures 6 (8, 9½)"/15 (20.5, 24)cm from beg, end with a WS row.

ARMHOLE SHAPING
Bind off 6 sts at beg of next 2 rows—48

Gauge
20 sts and 30 rows to 4"/10cm over lace pat using larger needles.
Take time to check gauge.

53 Lace Pullover

(56, 64) sts.
Cont in lace pat until armhole measures
4 (4½, 5)"/10 (11.5, 12.5)cm, end with a
WS row.

NECK AND SHOULDER SHAPING
Next row (RS) Work 14 (17, 20) sts
in pat, place center 20 (22, 24) sts on
holder for back neck, join a 2nd ball of
yarn and work in pat to end of row.
Working both sides at once with separate
balls of yarn, dec 1 st at each neck edge
every WS row twice—12 (15, 18) sts rem
each side for shoulder.
Bind off 6 (7, 9) sts from each shoulder
edge once, then bind off rem 6 (8, 9) sts.

Front
Work as for back until armhole measures
3 (3½, 4)"/7.5 (9, 10)cm, end with a WS row.

NECK AND SHOULDER SHAPING
Next row (RS) Work 19 (22, 25) sts
in pat, place center 10 (12, 14) sts on
holder for front neck, join a 2nd ball of
yarn and work in pat to end of row.
Working both sides at once with
separate balls of yarn, bind off 2 sts at
each neck edge once, then bind off 1 st
at each neck edge 5 times—12 (15, 18)
sts rem each side for shoulder. Cont in pat
until armhole measures same as back to
shoulders. Shape shoulders as for back.

Sleeves
With smaller needles and A, cast on 36 sts.
Row 1 (WS) K3, *p6, k2; rep from * to
last st, k1.
Row 2 P3, *k6, p2; rep from * to last st, p1.
Rep last 2 rows four times more, then
row 1 once, end with a WS row.

BEGIN LACE PATTERN
Beg with row 1 and work in lace pat,
AT THE SAME TIME, inc 1 st each side
of first row and then every 12th (10th,
10th) row 4 (6, 8) times more, working
inc sts into pat—46 (50, 54) sts.
Work even until piece measures 8½
(10½, 11½)"/21.5 (26.5, 29)cm from
beg, end with a WS row. Place marker
each edge of last row. Work even in pat
until 10 rows have been worked above
markers. Bind off in pat.

Finishing
Weave in ends and block to measurements.
Sew shoulder seams. Sew top edge of
sleeve cap to straight edge of armhole,
then sew side edges of sleeve above

markers to bound-off sts of armhole.
Sew side and sleeve seams.

NECKBAND
With RS facing, circular needle, and
A, pick up and k 70 (74, 78) sts evenly
around neck edge, including sts on
holder. Join and pm for beg of rnd. Knit
3 rnds. Bind off all sts loosely knitwise.

HEM EDGING
With RS facing and crochet hook, join B
with a sl st to cast-on edge at side seam.
Work sc evenly around lower edge.
Join with a sl st to first sc. Fasten off.

SLEEVE EDGING
Work as for hem edging. ■

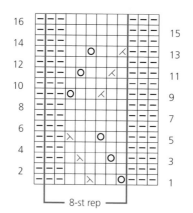

STITCH KEY

☐ k on RS, p on WS

─ p on RS, k on WS

O yo

⊠ k2tog

⊠ ssk

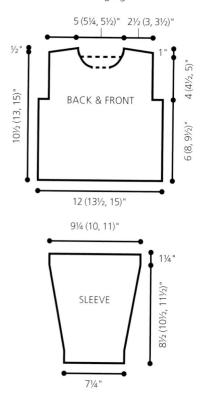

Cabled Blanket

A clever cable pattern makes this blanket reversible, and chunky yarn makes it a quick, fun knit.

DESIGNED BY LOIS S. YOUNG

Knitted Measurements
32 x 36"/81 x 91.5cm

Materials
- 9 3½oz/100g skeins (each approx 120yd/110m) of Cascade Yarns *Pacific Chunky* (acrylic/superwash merino wool) in #93 Methyl Blue (5)
- One each sizes 9 and 10 (5.5 and 6mm) circular needle, 32"/80cm long, *or size to obtain gauge*
- Cable needle (cn)
- Removable stitch marker

Notes
1) Pattern is reversible. Place a removable stitch marker at the right edge of piece to designate RS of work.
2) When cable is turned, knit stitches are converted to purl stitches and vice versa.
3) Circular needles are used to accommodate the large number of sts. Do *not* join. Work back and forth in rows.

Cable Pattern
(over a multiple of 8 sts)
Row 1 (RS) K3, *k2, p2, sl 2 sts to cn and hold to *front* of work, k2, p2 from cn; rep from * to last 5 sts, k5.
Row 2 (WS) K3, *p2, k2; rep from * to last 5 sts, p2, k3.
Row 3 K3, *k2, p2; rep from * to last 5 sts, k5.
Row 4 Rep row 2.
Rep rows 1–4 for cable pat.

Blanket
With smaller needle, loosely cast on 160 sts. Knit 5 rows. Change to larger needle. Work in cable pat until piece measures approx 35"/89cm from beg, end with a row 1 of pat.
Change to smaller needle. Knit 4 rows. Bind off knitwise on WS row.

Finishing
Weave in ends. Block to measurements. ■

Gauge
20 sts and 20 rows to 4"/10cm over cable pat using larger needle.
Take time to check gauge.

Butterfly Bolero

With its all-over butterfly stitch pattern, this pretty cropped jacket is a perfect topper for any frock.

DESIGNED BY YOKO HATTA

Sizes

Instructions are written for sizes 2 (4, 6). Shown in size 4.

Knitted Measurements

Chest (closed) 26 (28, 29½)"/66 (71, 75)cm
Length 8½ (9½, 10½)"/21.5 (24, 26.5)cm
Upper arm 9¾ (11, 12)"/25 (28, 30.5)cm

Materials

- 2 (2, 3) 3½oz/100g skeins (each approx 213yd/195m) of Cascade Yarns *Pacific* (acrylic/superwash merino wool) in #18 Cotton Candy (4)
- One each sizes 4 and 6 (3.5 and 4mm) needles, *or size to obtain gauge*
- Cable needle (cn)
- Stitch markers
- Stitch holders
- One ¹¹/₁₆"/18mm button

Stitch Glossary

2-St RT Sl 1 st to cn and hold to *back*, k1, k1 from cn.
2-St LT Sl 1 st to cn and hold to *front*, k1, k1 from cn.

3-Needle Bind-Off

1) Hold right sides of pieces together on two needles. Insert third needle knitwise into first st on each needle and wrap yarn knitwise.
2) Knit these two sts together and drop them from the needles. *Knit the next two sts together in the same manner.
3) Pass first st on third needle over second st and off needle. Rep from * in step 2 across row until all sts are bound off.

Back

With smaller needles, cast on 71 (76, 81) sts.
Knit 6 rows.
Change to larger needles.

BEGIN BUTTERFLY STITCH CHART
Rows 1–5 Work even in St st (k on RS, p on WS).
Note For chart row 6 (WS), chart begins with st 21 (26, 21) and ends at st 1.
Chart row 6 (WS) P1 (6, 1), *p1, [p1, wrapping yarn twice around needle] twice, p7; rep from * to end.

Cont to foll chart in this way through row 13, then rep rows 2–13 of chart until piece measures 8 (9, 10)"/20.5 (23, 25.5)cm from beg.
On last WS, pm to mark the center 13 (14, 15) sts.

NECK SHAPING
Next row (RS) Work to the center marked sts, join a 2nd ball of yarn and bind off center 13 (14, 15) sts, work to end. Working both sides at once, bind

Gauge

22 sts and 29 rows to 4"/10cm over chart pat using larger needles.
Take time to check gauge.

Butterfly Bolero

off 3 sts from each neck edge once, then 2 sts once. Place rem 24 (26, 28) sts on st holders each side for shoulders.

Left Front
With smaller needles, cast on 37 (40, 44) sts. Knit 6 rows.
Change to larger needles.

BEGIN BUTTERFLY STITCH CHART
Row 1 (RS) Knit.
Row 2 (WS) K4 (for front band), p to end.
Rows 3 and 5 Knit.
Row 4 Rep row 2.
Note For chart row 6 (WS), chart begins with st 23 (26, 20) and ends at st 1.
Chart row 6 (WS) K4, p3 (6, 0), *p1, [p1 st, wrapping yarn twice around needle] twice, p7; rep from * to end. Cont to foll chart, with 4-st front band in garter st (k every row), until piece measures 5½ (6½, 7½,)"/14 (16.5, 19)cm from beg, end with a RS row.

NECK SHAPING
Next row (WS) Bind off 8 (8, 9) sts, work to end.
Cont to shape neck by binding off 2 sts from neck edge on next WS row. Then, dec 1 st at neck edge on the next 3 (4, 5) RS rows—24 (26, 28) sts. Work even until piece measures same length as back.

Right Front
With smaller needles, cast on 37 (40, 44) sts. Knit 6 rows.
Change to larger needles.

BEGIN BUTTERFLY STITCH CHART
Row 1 (RS) Knit.
Row 2 (WS) P to last 4 sts, k4 (for front band).
Rows 3 and 5 Knit.
Row 4 Rep row 2.

Chart row 6 (WS) P6, *p1, [p1, wrapping yarn twice around needle] twice, p7; rep from * to last 4 sts, k4. Cont to foll chart, with 4-st front band in garter st, until piece measures 5¼ (6¼, 7¼)"/13.5 (16, 18.5)cm from beg.
Buttonhole row (RS) K2, yo, k2tog, work to end. Work even for 1 row more.

NECK SHAPING
Next row (RS) Bind off 8 (8, 9) sts, work to end. Cont to shape neck by binding off 2 sts from neck edge on next RS row. Then, dec 1 st at neck edge on the next 3 (4, 5) RS rows—24 (26, 28) sts. Complete same as left front.

Sleeves
With smaller needles, cast on 32 (36, 40) sts. Knit 6 rows.
Change to larger needles.

BEGIN BUTTERFLY STITCH CHART
Rows 1–4 Work even in St st.
Inc row 5 (RS) K1, kfb, work to last 2 sts, kfb, k1—34 (38, 42) sts.
Row 6 (WS) P5 (7, 8), *p1, [p1, wrapping yarn twice around needle] twice, p7; rep from *, end last rep p7 (9, 2).

Cont to foll chart in this way through row 13, then rep rows 2–13 of chart. AT THE SAME TIME, rep inc row 5 (working inc sts into pat) every 4th row 8 (6, 5) times more, then every 6th row 2 (5, 7) times—54 (60, 66) sts. Work even until piece measures 8 (10, 11)"/20.5 (25.5, 28)cm from beg. Bind off.

Finishing
Block pieces to measurements. Join shoulders using 3-needle bind off. Place markers for sleeves 5 (5¼, 5½)"/12.5 (13.5, 14)cm down from shoulder seams on fronts and back. Sew top of sleeves to armholes between markers. Sew side and sleeve seams.

COLLAR
With smaller needles and RS facing, skip first 2 sts of right front band, pick up and k 17 (18, 19) sts along shaped right front neck edge, 23 (24, 25) sts along back neck edge, 17 (18, 19) sts along shaped left front neck edge, leaving last 2 sts of left front edge unworked—57 (60, 63) sts. Work in garter st for 18 rows. Bind off. Sew button opposite buttonhole. ■

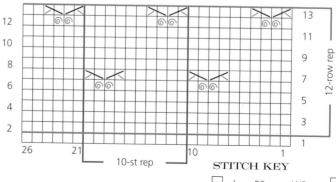

BUTTERFLY STITCH CHART

STITCH KEY

□ k on RS, p on WS   ⋈ 2-st RT

◎ p wrapping yarn   ⋈ 2-st LT
   twice around needle

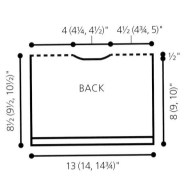

4 (4¼, 4½)" 4½ (4¾, 5)"

BACK

½"

8½ (9½, 10½)"

8 (9, 10)"

13 (14, 14¾)"

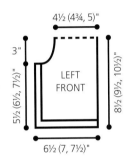

4½ (4¾, 5)"

3"

LEFT
FRONT

5½ (6½, 7½)"

8½ (9½, 10½)"

6½ (7, 7½)"

9¾ (11, 12)"

SLEEVE

8 (10, 11)"

6 (6½, 7¼)"

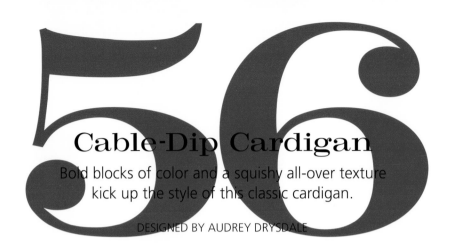

Cable-Dip Cardigan

Bold blocks of color and a squishy all-over texture
kick up the style of this classic cardigan.

DESIGNED BY AUDREY DRYSDALE

Sizes
Instructions are written for sizes 2 (4, 6).
Shown in size 2.

Knitted Measurements
Chest (closed) 24 (26, 28)"/61 (66, 71)cm
Length 13 (14½, 16)"/33 (37, 40.5)cm
Upper arm 10 (11, 12)"/25.5 (28, 30.5)cm

Materials
■ 2 (2, 3) 3½oz/100g skeins (each
approx 213yd/195m) of Cascade Yarns
Pacific (acrylic/superwash merino wool)
in #43 Ruby (A) (4)
■ 2 (3, 3) skeins in #24 Platinum (B)
■ One each sizes 6 and 8 (4 and 5mm)
circular needle, 29"/73.5cm long,
or size to obtain gauge
■ One pair each sizes 6 and 8 (4 and
5mm) needles
■ Cable needle (cn)
■ Stitch holders
■ Five ¹¹/₁₆"/17mm buttons

Note
Body is worked in one piece to the
underarms.

Stitch Glossary
6-st RC Sl 3 sts to cn and hold to *back*;
k3, k3 from cn.
6-st LC Sl 3 sts to cn and hold to *front*;
k3, k3 from cn.

Cable Pattern
(over a multiple of 6 sts plus 2)
Row 1 (RS) Knit.
Row 2 and all WS rows K1, p to last
st, k1.
Row 3 K1, *6-st RC; rep from * to last st, k1.
Rows 5 and 7 Knit.
Row 9 K4, *6-st LC; rep from * to last 4
sts, k4.
Row 11 Knit.
Row 12 Rep row 2.
Rep rows 1–12 for cable pat.

Body
With smaller circular needle and B, cast
on 138 (150, 162) sts. Do *not* join. Work
back and forth in garter st (k every row)
for 9 rows, end with a RS row.
Inc row (WS) Knit, inc 20 sts evenly
spaced—158 (170, 182) sts.
Change to larger circular needle.

BEGIN CABLE PATTERN
Rep rows 1–12 of cable pat 2 (2, 3)

times, then rows 1–6 for 0 (1, 0) times
more. Change to A. Beg with row 1 (7,
1), cont in cable pat until piece measures
7½ (8½, 9½)"/19 (21.5, 24)cm from beg,
end with a WS row.

DIVIDE FOR FRONTS AND BACK
Next row (RS) Work across first 38
(41, 44) sts, place these sts on holder
for right front, bind off next 5 sts for
right underarm, work until there are 72 (78,
84) sts on RH needle, leave these sts on
needle for back, bind off next 5 sts for left
underarm, work to end, place these last
38 (41, 44) sts on holder for left front.

Back
Change to larger straight needles. Cont
in cable pat as established until armhole
measures 5 (5½, 6)"/12.5 (14, 15)cm, end
with a WS row.

SHOULDER SHAPING
Bind off 9 (10, 11) sts at beg of next 2 rows,
then 10 (11, 12) sts at beg of next 2 rows.
Place rem 34 (36, 38) sts on holder for
back neck.

Left Front
Place 38 (41, 44) sts from left front

Gauge
27 sts and 28 rows to 4"/10cm over cable pat using larger needles. *Take time to check gauge.*

Cable-Dip Cardigan

holder onto larger straight needles ready for a WS row. Cont in cable pat as established until armhole measures 3½ (4, 4½)"/9 (10, 11.5)cm, end with a RS row.

NECK SHAPING
Bind off 12 (13, 14) sts at beg of next row. Dec 1 st from neck edge on next row, then *every* row 4 times more, then every other row twice—19 (21, 23) sts.
Work even until piece measures same length as back to shoulder, end with a WS row.

SHOULDER SHAPING
At armhole edge, bind off 9 (10, 11) sts once, then 10 (11, 12) sts once.

Right Front
Place 38 (41, 44) sts from right front holder onto larger straight needles ready for a WS row. Cont in cable pat as established until armhole measures 3½ (4, 4½)"/9 (10, 11.5)cm, end with a WS row.

NECK SHAPING
Bind off 12 (13, 14) sts at beg of next row. Dec 1 st from neck edge on next row, then *every* row 4 times more, then every other row twice—19 (21, 23) sts. Work even until piece measures same length as back to shoulder, end with a RS row.

SHOULDER SHAPING
From sholder edge, bind off 9 (10, 11) sts once, then 10 (11, 12) sts once.

Sleeves
With smaller straight needles and B, cast on 37 (40, 40) sts. Work in garter st for 9 rows, end with a RS row.
Inc row (WS) Knit, inc 13 (16, 16) sts evenly spaced—50 (56, 56) sts.
Change to larger needles.

BEGIN CABLE PATTERN
Rep rows 1–12 of cable pat 2 (2, 3) times, then rows 1–6 for 0 (1, 0) times more, then change to A and beg with row 1 (7, 1), cont in cable pat with A to end of piece. AT THE SAME TIME, after 12 (12, 6) rows have been worked in cable pat, inc 1 st each side (working inc sts into cable pat) on next row, then every 6th row 7 (8, 11) times more—66 (74, 80) sts.
Work even until piece measures 11 (13,14)"/28 (33, 35.5)cm from beg.
Bind off all sts.

Finishing
Block pieces to measurements. Sew shoulder and sleeve seams. Set in sleeves, sewing top ½"/1.5cm of sleeve along bound-off edge of armhole.

BUTTONBAND
With smaller straight needles and B, cast on 7 sts. Work in garter st until piece measures same height as B section of left front edge (when slightly stretched), end with a WS row. Cut B. With A, cont in garter st and work until piece measures same height as left front edge to neck edge (when slightly stretched), end with a WS row. Place 7 sts on holder.

Sew buttonband to left front edge, matching up color changes.
Place markers for 4 buttons on buttonband, with the first ½"/1.5cm from lower edge and last 1¾"/4.5cm from neck edge and 2 spaced evenly between; the 5th button will be on neckband.

BUTTONHOLE BAND
Work as for buttonband, while AT THE SAME TIME working buttonholes opposite markers as follows:
Buttonhole row 1 (RS) K2, bind off next 2 sts, k3.
Buttonhole row 2 K3, cast on 2 sts, k2.

NECKBAND
With RS facing, smaller straight needles and A, k 7 sts from buttonhole band holder, pick up and k 23 (24, 25) sts along right neck edge, k 34 (36, 38) sts from back neck holder dec 6 sts evenly spaced, pick up and k 23 (24, 25) sts along left neck edge, k 7 sts from buttonband holder—88 (92, 96) sts. Knit 5 rows. Rep buttonhole rows 1 and 2 as for buttonhole band, knitting to end after binding off sts. Knit 3 rows.
Bind off all sts knitwise.
Sew buttons opposite buttonholes. ∎

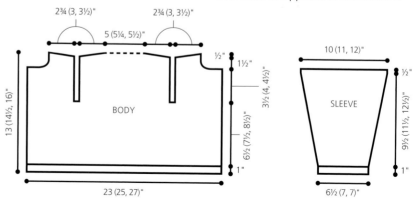

57

Striped Tunic

Colorful stripes turn this simple tunic into a fabulous frock.
Pair it with patterned leggings for an extra-fun look.

DESIGNED BY CAARIN FLEISCHMANN

Sizes
Instructions are written for sizes 2 (4, 6).
Shown in size 4.

Knitted Measurements
Chest 25 (26½, 29)"/63.5 (67.5, 73.5)cm
Length 15¼ (16¼, 18¾)"/39 (41, 47.5)cm
Upperarm 7 (7½, 8½)"/18 (19, 21.5)cm

Materials
■ 2 (3, 3) 3½oz/100g skeins (each
approx 213yd/195m) of Cascade Yarns
Pacific (acrylic/superwash merino wool)
in #106 Carmine Rose (A) ⬤
■ 2 skeins in #84 Persimmon (B)
■ One each sizes 5 and 6 (3.75 and
4mm) circular needle, 24"/60cm long,
or size to obtain gauge
■ One set (5) each sizes 5 and 6 (3.75
and 4mm) double-pointed needles (dpn)
■ Stitch markers
■ Stitch holder

Notes
1) Tunic is worked in the round from the
top down.
2) Sleeves are worked in the round using
double-pointed needles.
3) Row gauge is critical if correct length
of garment is to be achieved.

Stitch Glossary
M1R (make 1 right) Insert LH needle from
back to front under the strand between
last st worked and next st on LH needle.
K into the front loop to twist the st.
M1L (make 1 left) Insert LH needle from
front to back under the strand between last
st worked and next st on LH needle. K into
the back loop to twist the st.

Stripe Pattern
Worked in St st (k every rnd) as foll:
[19 (20, 23) rnds A, 19 (20, 23) rnds B]
twice, 19 (20, 23) rnds A.

Tunic
Beg at the neck edge, with smaller
circular needle and B, cast on 58 (64, 70)
sts. Join, being careful not to twist sts,
and pm for beg of rnd.
Next rnd Knit.
Change to larger circular needle and beg
stripe pat, working as foll:
Next rnd Purl.
Set-up rnd K1 (armhole st), pm, k6
(7, 8) for right sleeve, pm, k1 (armhole
st), pm, k21 (23, 25) for front, pm, k1
(armhole st), pm, k6 (7, 8) for left sleeve,
pm, k1 (armhole st), pm, k21 (23, 25)
for back.
Rnd 1 Purl.
Inc rnd [K1, sm, M1R, k to marker, M1L,
sm] 4 times—8 sts inc'd for armholes.
Next rnd Knit.
Rep last 2 rnds 7 (8, 10) times more—
122 (136, 158) sts.
Inc rnd K to marker before front sts, sm,
M1R, k to next marker, M1L, sm, k1, sm,
k to marker before back sts, sm, M1R,

Gauge
20 sts and 26 rnds to 4"/10cm over St st using larger needles.
Take time to check gauge.

Striped Tunic

k to next marker, M1L, sm, k1, sm—4 sts inc'd for armholes.
Next rnd Knit.
Inc rnd [K1, sm, M1R, k to marker, M1L, sm] 4 times—8 sts inc'd for armholes.
Next rnd Knit.
Rep last 4 rnds four times more—182 (196, 218) sts.

DIVIDE FOR BODY AND SLEEVES
Note Make note of where you are in the stripe pattern for the sleeves, and remove markers as you come to them on the first row.
Rnd 1 (RS) Transfer first 32 (35, 40) sts to holder for right sleeve, cast on 3 sts, k59 (63, 69) sts for front, transfer next 32 (35, 40) sts to holder for left sleeve, cast on 3 sts, k59 (63, 69) sts for back—124 (132, 144) sts for body.
Cont in St st and stripe pat until 16 (17, 20) rnds of final stripe have been worked. Body measures approx 8 (8½, 10½)"/20.5 (21.5, 26.5)cm from dividing row.
Change to smaller circular needles.
Next rnd Purl.

Next rnd Knit.
Rep last 2 rnds twice more. Bind off all sts purlwise.

Sleeves
Keeping stripe pat to match body, with larger dpn, pick up and k 1 st from underarm, pm, pick up and k 1 st from underarm, k32 (35, 40) sleeve sts, pick up and k 1 st, pm, join to work in rnds—35 (38, 43) sts. Work 10 rnds in St st and stripe pat.
Dec rnd K1, sm, k2tog, k to last 3 sts, ssk, k1—2 sts dec'd.
Knit 13 (11, 11) rnds.
Rep last 14 (12, 12) rnds 2 (3, 4) times more—29 (30, 33) sts. Work even until last rnd of stripe pat has been worked.
Sleeve measures approx 8½ (9, 10¾)"/21.5 (23, 27.5)cm from dividing row.
Change to smaller dpn.
Cut A and cont with B.
Next rnd Purl.
Next rnd Knit. Bind off all sts purlwise.

Finishing
Weave in ends. Block to measurements. ■

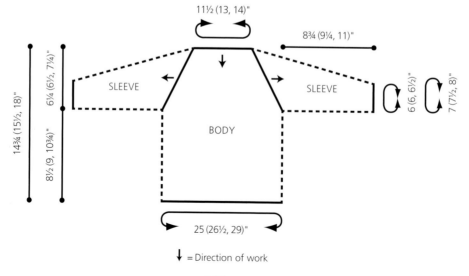

11½ (13, 14)"

8¾ (9¼, 11)"

14¾ (15½, 18)"

6¼ (6½, 7¼)"

8½ (9, 10¾)"

SLEEVE

SLEEVE

BODY

6 (6, 6½)"

7 (7½, 8)"

25 (26½, 29)"

↓ = Direction of work

58

Flower Hat

A pretty button and a knitted blossom embellish this simple beanie,
knit seamlessly in the round.

DESIGNED BY LISA CRAIG

Knitted Measurements
Brim circumference 16"/40.5cm
Length 8"/20.5cm

Materials
■ 1 3½oz/100g skeins (each approx
213yd/195m) of Cascade Yarns *Pacific*
(acrylic/superwash merino wool)
in #52 Geranium 〔4〕
■ One set (5) each sizes 7 and 8 (4.5
and 5mm) double-pointed needles (dpn),
or size to obtain gauge
■ Stitch marker
■ One ¾"/19mm button

Hat
With smaller dpn, cast on 88 sts. Divide
sts evenly over 4 needles. Join, taking care
not to twist sts, and pm for beg of rnd.
Rnd 1 *K2, p2; rep from * around.
Rep rnd 1 for k2, p2 rib for 2"/5cm.
Change to larger dpn.
Knit 1 rnd, purl 1 rnd.
Work 5 rnds in St st (k every rnd).
Purl 1 rnd, knit 1 rnd, purl 1 rnd.
Work even in St st until hat measures
4¾"/12cm from beg.

CROWN SHAPING
Dec rnd 1 *K2tog, k9; rep from *

around—80 sts.
Rnd 2 and all even rnds to rnd 16 Knit.
Dec rnd 3 *K2tog, k8; rep from *
around—72 sts.
Dec rnd 5 *K2tog, k7; rep from *
around—64 sts.
Dec rnd 7 *K2tog, k6; rep from *
around—56 sts.
Dec rnd 9 *K2tog, k5; rep from *
around—48 sts.
Dec rnd 11 *K2tog, k4; rep from *
around—40 sts.

Dec rnd 13 *K2tog, k3; rep from *
around—32 sts.
Dec rnd 15 *K2tog, k2; rep from *
around—24 sts.
Dec rnd 17 *K2tog, k1; rep from *
around—16 sts.
Dec rnd 18 *K2tog; rep from *
around—8 sts.
Cut yarn and pull through rem sts, draw
up and secure.

Flower
With smaller dpn, cast on 3 sts.
Row 1 Knit.
Row 2 Cast on 3 sts, k to end—6 sts.
Rows 3, 4, and 5 Knit.
Row 6 Sl 1, k3, lift 2nd, 3rd, and 4th sts
on RH needle over first st and off, k2—3 sts.
Rep rows 1–6 five times more. Bind off,
leaving a long tail.
Draw tail through sts along straight edge
of piece and draw up tightly to form center
of flower. Sew bound-off edge to cast-on
edge. Sew button to center of flower
and sew flower to hat so that lower edge
is just above first purl ridge, using photo
as guide.

Finishing
Weave in ends. ■

Gauge
20 sts and 24 rnds to 4"/10cm over St st using larger needles.
Take time to check gauge.

Color-Block Hoodie

Bold colors, a kangaroo pocket, and a cozy hood will make this everyday pullover a special favorite.

DESIGNED BY CHERYL MURRAY

Sizes
Instructions are written for sizes 2 (4, 6). Shown in size 4.

Knitted Measurements
Chest 24 (26, 29)"/61 (66, 73.5)cm
Length 14½ (16¼, 17¾)"/37 (41, 45)cm
Upperarm 9 (10, 10½)"/23 (25.5, 26.5)cm

Materials
- 3 (3, 4) 3½oz/100g skeins (each approx 120yd/110m) of Cascade Yarns *Pacific Chunky* (acrylic/superwash merino wool) in #34 Pewter (A) ⑤
- 2 skeins #92 Blue Mist (B)
- One each sizes 9 and 10 (5.5 and 6mm) circular needle, 24"/60cm long, *or size to obtain gauge*
- One set (5) each sizes 9 and 10 (5.5 and 6mm) double-pointed needles (dpn)
- Stitch markers
- Stitch holders

Notes
1) Hoodie is worked in the round from the lower edge to armhole.
2) Sleeves are worked in the round using dpn to armhole. If desired, you may then transfer sts to a circular needle to work back and forth in rows.

K1, P1 Rib
(over an even number of sts)
Rnd 1 *K1, p1; rep from * around.
Rep rnd 1 for k1, p1 rib.

Stitch Glossary
M1R (make 1 right) Insert left needle from *back to front* into the horizontal strand between the last st worked and the next st on left needle. K into the front loop to twist the st.
M1L (make 1 left) Insert left needle from *front to back* into the horizontal strand between the last st worked and the next st on left needle. K into the back loop to twist the st.

3-Needle Bind-off
1) Divide sts evenly between two needles and hold RS together.
2) Insert third needle knitwise into first st on each needle and knit these two sts together, dropping them from the LH needles. *Knit the next two sts together in the same manner.
3) Pass first st on third needle over second st and off needle. Rep from * in step 2 across row until all sts are bound off.

Hoodie
With smaller circular needle and A, cast on 90 (98, 108) sts. Join, being careful not to twist sts, and pm for beg of rnd. Work 4 rnds in k1, p1 rib.
Change to larger circular needle and work in St st (knit every rnd) until piece measures 8 (9½, 10½)"/20.5 (24, 26.5)cm from beg.

DIVIDE FOR FRONT AND BACK
Next rnd K42 (45, 50), bind off next 6 (8, 8) sts, k to last 3 (4, 4) sts before beg of rnd marker, bind off next 6 (8, 8) sts, removing marker. Place last 39 (41, 46) sts on holder for front.
Work on rem 39 (41, 46) sts for back as foll:

RAGLAN SHAPING
Dec row (RS) K1, k2tog, k to last 3 sts, ssk, k1—37 (39, 44) sts.
Rep dec row every other row 9 (8, 9) times more, then every 4th row 2 (3, 3) times—15 (17, 20) sts. Bind off rem sts.

Front
Place 39 (41, 46) sts from front holder onto needle, ready for a RS row. Join yarn and pm on each side of center 5 (5, 6) sts.
Work raglan shaping as for back and, AT THE SAME TIME, when front measures 10 (11¼, 12½)"/25.5 (28.5, 32)cm from beg, bind off center 5 (5, 6) sts and cont

Gauge
15 sts and 20 rnds/rows to 4"/10cm over St st using larger needles. *Take time to check gauge.*

Color-Block Hoodie

each side with a separate ball of yarn—5 (6, 7) sts rem each side after shaping is completed. Bind off rem sts each side.

Sleeves

With smaller dpn and A, cast on 24 (26, 28) sts. Divide sts evenly between 4 needles. Join and pm for beg of rnd. Purl 5 rnds. Change to larger dpn. With B, knit 5 rnds.
Inc rnd K1, M1R, k to last st, M1L, k1—26 (28, 30) sts.
Cont in St st, rep inc rnd every 6th rnd 4 (5, 5) times more—34 (38, 40) sts.
Work even until piece measures 8½ (9½, 11½)"/21.5 (24, 29)cm from beg.
Next rnd K to last 3 (4, 4) sts, bind off next 6 (8, 8) sts, removing marker—28 (30, 32) sts. Cont back and forth in rows as foll:

RAGLAN SHAPING

Dec row (RS) K1, k2tog, k to last 3 sts, ssk, k1—26 (28, 30) sts.
Rep dec row every other row 9 (10, 9) times more, then every 4th row 2 (2, 3) times—4 (4, 6) sts. Bind off rem sts.

Finishing

Weave in ends and block to measurements. Sew raglan, sleeve, and side seams.

HOOD

With RS facing, larger circular needle, and B, pick up and k 30 (34, 42) sts evenly around neck edge. Do *not* join. Work back and forth in rows. Beg with a WS (knit) row, work 5 rows in Rev St st (k on WS, p on RS), end with a WS row. Cut B and join A.
Next row (RS) K14 (16, 20), pm, k2, pm, k14 (16, 20).
Work 3 rows in St st.
Inc row (RS) K to marker, M1R, sm, k2, sm, M1L, k to end—32 (36, 44) sts.

Cont in St st (k on RS, p on WS), working inc row every 4th row 6 times more, then every 6th row twice—48 (52, 60) sts. Work even until hood measures 9 (9, 10)"/23 (23, 25.5)cm from pick-up row, end with a WS row. Cut A and join B. Work 2 rows in Rev St st. Slip first 24 (26, 30) sts to spare needle. Join top of hood seam using larger dpn for 3-needle bind-off.

HOOD AND PLACKET EDGING

With RS facing, smaller circular needle, and B, pick up and k 13 (15, 15) sts along right front placket opening, 69 (69, 77) sts along hood edge, 13 (15, 15) sts along left front placket opening—95 (99, 107) sts. Do *not* join. Work back and forth in rows. Beg with a WS (knit) row, work 4 rows in Rev St st, end with a RS row. Bind off loosely knitwise. Sew sides of edging to bound-off sts at center front.

POCKET

With 2 larger dpn and A, cast on 26 sts. Work 4 rows in St st, end with a WS row.
Dec row (RS) K1, k2tog, k to last 3 sts, ssk, k1—24 sts.
Rep dec row every 4th row 4 times more—16 sts.
Work even in St st until piece measures 5½"/14cm from beg, end with a WS row. Bind off all sts.

POCKET EDGING

With larger dpn, RS facing and B, pick up and k 19 sts evenly along side edge of pocket. Beg with a WS (knit) row, work 5 rows in Rev St st, end with a WS row. Bind off loosely purlwise.
Rep for rem side edge.
Center pocket on front of sweater, approx 1½"/4cm up from lower edge. Sew lower and top edges in place, leaving sides open for pocket opening. ■

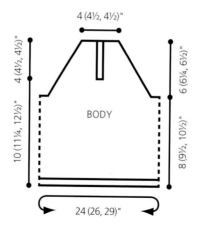

4 (4½, 4½)"

4 (4½, 4½)"

10 (11¼, 12½)"

6 (6¼, 6½)"

8 (9½, 10½)"

BODY

24 (26, 29)"

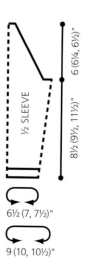

6 (6¼, 6½)"

½ SLEEVE

8½ (9½, 11½)"

6½ (7, 7½)"

9 (10, 10½)"

60

Red Riding Cape

With its warm collar and fun I-cord ties,
this gorgeous textured cape can make any time dress-up time.

DESIGNED BY SARAH THIENEMAN

Sizes
Instructions are written for sizes 2 (4, 6).
Shown in size 6.

Knitted Measurements
Length (lower edge to collar) 14½
(15½, 18)"/37 (39.5, 46)cm
Width (lower edge) 32½ (33½,
35)"/82.5 (85, 89)cm

Materials
■ 2 (3, 3) 3½oz/100g skeins (each
approx 213yd/195m) of Cascade Yarns
Pacific (acrylic/superwash merino wool)
in #36 Christmas Red (4)
■ One size 6 (4mm) circular needle,
24"/60cm long, *or size to obtain gauges*
■ Two size 6 (4mm) double-pointed
needles (dpn), for I-cord
■ Cable needle (cn)

Stitch Glossary
6-st LC Sl 3 sts to cn and hold to *front*,
k3, k3 from cn.
6-st RC Sl 3 sts to cn and hold to *back*,
k3, k3 from cn.

Note
Circular needle is used on the body to
accommodate the large number of sts. Do

not join. Work back and forth in rows.

Quilted Stitch
(over a multiple of 6 sts plus 2)
Row 1 (WS) P1, *yo, p5, yo, p1; rep
from * to last st, p1.
Row 2 K1, *sl 1 dropping yo, k4, sl 1
dropping yo; rep from * to last st, k1.

Rows 3 and 5 P1, *sl 1, p4, sl 1; rep
from * to last st, p1.
Row 4 K1, *sl 1, k4, sl 1; rep from * to
last st, k1.
Row 6 K1, *drop next st to front of
work, k2, k dropped st, sl 2, drop next st
to front of work, place last 2 sl sts back
onto LH needle, k dropped st, k2; rep
from * to last st, k1.
Row 7 P1, *p2, [yo, p1] twice, p2; rep
from * to last st, p1.
Row 8 K1, *k2, [sl 1 dropping yo] twice,
k2; rep from * to last st, k1.
Rows 9 and 11 P1, *p2, sl 2, p2; rep
from * to last st, p1.
Row 10 K1, *k2, sl 2, k2; rep from * to
last st, k1.
Row 12 K1, *sl 2, drop next st to front
of work, place last 2 sl sts back onto LH
needle, k dropped st, k2, drop next st to
front of work, k2, k dropped st; rep from
* to last st, k1.
Rep rows 1–12 for quilted st.

Cable Panel
(over 9 sts)
Row 1 and all WS rows Purl.
Rows 2 and 6 Knit.
Row 4 6-st LC, k3.

Gauges
22 sts and 36 rows to 4"/10cm over garter st using size 6 (4mm) needles.
23 sts and 32 rows to 4"/10cm over quilted st using size 6 (4mm) needles. *Take time to check gauges.*

Row 8 K3, 6-st RC.
Row 9 Purl.
Rep rows 2–9 for cable panel.

Cape
Beg at the lower edge, cast on 178 (184, 190) sts. Work 15 rows in garter st (k every row), end with a RS row.

BEGIN PATTERNS
Row 1 (WS) K12 (15, 15), work 20 sts in quilted st, k6 (6, 7), work 9 sts of cable panel, k6 (6, 7), work 20 sts in quilted st, k5 (5, 6), work 9 sts of cable panel, k4, work 9 sts of cable panel, k5 (5, 6), work 20 sts in quilted st, k6 (6, 7), work 9 sts of cable panel, k6 (6, 7), work 20 sts in quilted st, k12 (15, 15).
Row 2 K12 (15, 15), work 20 sts in quilted st, p6 (6, 7), work 9 sts of cable panel, p6 (6, 7), work 20 sts in quilted st, p5 (5, 6), work 9 sts of cable panel, p4, work 9 sts of cable panel, p5 (5, 6), work 20 sts in quilted st, p6 (6, 7), work 9 sts of cable panel, p6 (6, 7), work 20 sts in quilted st, k12 (15, 15).
Cont in pats as established until piece measures 12½ (13½, 16)"/32 (34.5, 40.5)cm from beg, end with a RS row.

SHOULDER SHAPING
Note When working decs across quilted st pat and cable panel, maintain pat as much as possible until all decs are completed, then resume in pat.
Dec row (WS) K2, [k2tog] 4 (5, 5) times, k2 (3, 3), [p2tog] 3 times, work 8 sts in pat, [p2tog] 3 times, k2tog, k2 (2, 3),

k2tog, work 9 sts in pat, k2tog, k2 (2, 3), k2tog, [p2tog] 3 times, work 8 sts in pat, [p2tog] 3 times, k2tog, k1 (1, 2), k2tog, [p2tog] 11 times, k2tog, k1 (1, 2), k2tog, [p2tog] 3 times, work 8 sts in pat, [p2tog] 3 times, k2tog, k2 (2, 3), k2tog, work 9 sts in pat, k2tog, k2 (2, 3), k2tog, [p2tog] 3 times, work 8 sts in pat, [p2tog] 3 times, k2 (3, 3), [k2tog] 4 (5, 5) times, k2—123 (127, 133) sts.
Next row (RS) K8 (10, 10), work 14 sts in quilted st, p4 (4, 5), work 9 sts of cable panel, p4 (4, 5), work 14 sts in quilted st, p3 (3, 4), k1, work 9 sts in cable panel, k1, p 3 (3, 4), work 14 sts in quilted st, p4 (4, 5), work 9 sts in cable panel, p4 (4, 5), work 14 sts in quilted st, k8 (10, 10).
Dec row (WS) [K2tog] 4 (5, 5) times, [p2tog] twice, work 6 sts in pat, [p2tog] twice, [k2tog] twice, k0 (0, 1), work 9 sts in pat, k0 (0, 1), [k2tog] twice, [p2tog] twice, work 6 sts in pat, [p2tog] twice, [k2tog] 1 (1, 2) times, k1 (1, 0), p2tog, p7, p2tog, k1 (1, 0), [k2tog] 1 (1, 2) times, [p2tog] twice, work 6 sts in pat, [p2tog] twice, [k2tog] twice, k0 (0, 1), work 9 sts in pat, k0 (0, 1), [k2tog] twice, [p2tog] twice, work 6 sts in pat, [p2tog] twice, [k2tog] 4 (5, 5) times—87 (89, 93) sts.
Next row K4 (5, 5), work 10 sts in quilted st, p2 (2, 3), work 9 sts of cable panel, p2 (2, 3), work 10 sts in quilted st, p2, work 9 sts in cable panel, p2, work 10 sts in quilted st, p2 (2, 3), work 9 sts in cable panel, p2 (2, 3), work 10 sts in quilted st, k4 (5, 5)
Dec row K4 (5, 5), p2tog, work 6 sts in pat,

p2tog, k2 (2, 1), [k2tog] 0 (0, 1) times, work 9 sts in pat, [k2tog] 0 (0, 1) times, k2 (2, 1), p2tog, work 6 sts in pat, p2tog, k2, work 9 sts in pat, k2, p2tog, work 6 sts in pat, p2tog, k2 (2, 1), [k2tog] 0 (0, 1) times, work 9 sts in pat, [k2tog] 0 (0, 1) times, k2 (2, 1), p2tog, work 6 sts in pat, p2tog, k4 (5, 5)—79 (81, 81) sts.
Cont even in pat until piece measures 14½ (15½, 18)"/37 (39.5, 46)cm from beg, end with a WS row.

COLLAR
Work 5 rows in garter st, end with a RS row.
Eyelet row (WS) K10, [yo twice, k20] 3 times, yo twice, k9 (11, 11).
Next row Knit, working k1 into double yo—83 (85, 85) sts.
Work 4 rows more in garter st, end with a RS row. Bind off all sts knitwise.

Finishing
Weave in ends and block to measurements.

I-CORD TIES (MAKE 2)
With dpn, cast on 3 sts.
*Row 1 (RS) Knit. Slide sts back to beg of needle to work next row from the RS. Bring yarn around from back. Rep from * until I-cord measures 25"/63.5cm.
Cut yarn, leaving a long tail, and draw tail through open sts to fasten off.
Holding both I-cords together, lightly twist and knot together at ends.
Weave twisted cords through eyelet holes at collar. ■

index